CARPENTERS OF LIGHT

CARPENTERS OF LIGHT

Some Contemporary English Poets

NEIL POWELL

BARNES & NOBLE

BOOKS

10 East 53d St., New York 10022
(a division of Harper & Row Publishers, Inc.)

Published in the United States of America 1980 by
HARPER & ROW PUBLISHERS, INC.
BARNES & NOBLE IMPORT DIVISION
ISBN 0-06-495665-2
Library of Congress catalog card number LC 79-54320

Printed in Great Britain by
Billings, Guildford

For Alan Hurd and Martin Wright

And will the poet, carpenter of light,
    Work with the grain henceforward?
                     (Donald Davie, 'With the Grain')

CONTENTS

PREFACE

The arrangement of this book is very straightforward. What I have attempted to do is to examine the work of a number of contemporary poets in the light of an English tradition which I try to define in my first chapter. In this first chapter, 'What is "Traditional" Poetry?', I deal with some ideas of traditionalism and modernism as discussed by three critics closely concerned with the poetry of this century — Graham Hough, Donald Davie, and Yvor Winters — in order to provide a context and a terminology of contemporary traditionalism. I then go on to consider the poetry of Thom Gunn, which seems to me a particularly striking example of the quest for a contemporary version of what Winters calls the 'plain style', Donald Davie, and Philip Larkin. The remaining chapters deal with the conflict of orthodoxies in English poetry during the nineteen-sixties and, briefly, with some other recent poets whose work is more or less 'traditional'.

Carpenters of Light is largely based upon a thesis entitled *Tradition and Structure in Contemporary Poetry*, which I started as a postgraduate student at the University of Warwick between 1969 and 1971, and eventually submitted in 1974. The first chapter survives, basically unchanged, and it may retain a rather self-consciously thesis-like tone. The rest of the book has been substantially revised and in places entirely reorganised. I have tried throughout to incorporate footnotes, which are a research student's best friends but which can be maddening to the reader, into the text: my original, somewhat shorter chapter on Gunn, for example, had 87 footnotes, which now strikes me as impressive but excessive.

Some of the material included here has been previously published — in the form of essays and book reviews — in *Critical Quarterly, Phoenix, PN Review, Tracks,* and *The Use of English.*

My debts to other writers are, I hope, adequately recorded in the text and the bibliography. I am grateful to Peter Porter for his permission to quote from a letter to me in Chapter Five, and to the writers who replied to a questionnaire on contemporary poetry which I sent to them on behalf of *Tracks* in 1970. I gladly record my thanks to unnamed teachers and friends at the University of Warwick, colleagues and students at Kimbolton School and St Christopher School, Letchworth; and I remember in particular conversations with Stuart Beeson, Martin Bennett, Bernard

Bergonzi, Martin Booth, Matthew Desmond, Jonty Driver, Roy Fuller, John Mole, Ben Ormerod, Peter Scupham, Rod Shand, Peter Smout, John Stratford, and John Sutton. Professor Bergonzi and George Fraser read and commented helpfully on the thesis as examiners. Michael Schmidt's editorial integrity and energy are well-known to Carcanet authors, who could not wish for a more serious and committed publisher. Finally, two special debts of gratitude. This book would not have existed without the long-standing interest and friendship of Alan Hurd, who taught me English — and encouraged me to write — at Sevenoaks School. Martin Wright, of the University of Warwick, persuaded me to read Winters and much else: I am grateful for his friendship and his scholarship and, not least, for his patience in reading and commenting on two drafts of *Tradition and Structure*. The errors and eccentricities of judgement are my own.

N.P.

Chapter One

WHAT IS TRADITIONAL POETRY?

1

GRAHAM HOUGH'S *Image and Experience* (1960) has been called 'the apologia of the Movement' (by C. B. Cox and A. R. Jones in 'After the Tranquilized Fifties', *Critical Quarterly*, VI, 2, summer 1964, p. 121); but in at least one respect this is misleading. None of the Movement poets is mentioned in the book, except Donald Davie, who is quoted once, with disapproval, as a critic, and whose *Articulate Energy* is briefly acknowledged in the Preface. *Image and Experience* — which consists of lectures and essays written during the 1950s — is not so much an apologia as a prophecy. Hough himself remarks that 'Crystal-gazing as a critical method had better be reduced to a minimum', but he did foresee a return to the 'main highway' of English poetry; his book is one which sets the stage but does not introduce the protagonists, so the background needs to be exceptionally convincing.

It is the first section of *Image and Experience,* 'Reflections on a Literary Revolution', which concerns me here; and a key passage occurs at the end of the second sub-section, 'Imagist Poetry and the Tradition':

> Then, if I were one of the morose depreciators of modern poetry that I fear I have often made myself sound like, I should proceed to say that the whole experiment had been a dead end, and that poetry must retrace its steps. But this is not what I want to say. If we are to use metaphors, mine would not be a cul-de-sac but a detour, a diversion from the main road. Traffic along the main road has been proceeding all the time, and we do not sufficiently remember this. In talking of modern poetry we ought to recall more often than we do that Hardy was writing till 1926, and that among the poets of our century are Robert Frost, Robert Graves, John Crowe Ransom, Edwin Muir and John Betjeman. But the detour has been considerable, and most of the heavy traffic has chosen to travel on it. It is probably time it rejoined the main highway. (p.56)[1]

The defect here is not in the argument but in the documentation. The 'main highway' represented by these poets would lead us into a back-water: none of them, except perhaps for Frost and Graves, could be

described as a poet of unquestionably major importance, and their tradi-
tionalism is of a restricted kind. But this is where the element of prophecy
reappears, for a more convincing alternative list would have included
poets whose reputations have greatly increased since Hough wrote his
book. It would include Auden, who is grouped inexplicably among the
difficult moderns; Empson, whose significance as a major influence on
the Movement had already been heralded by John Wain's essay on him in
the final number of *Penguin New Writing;*[2] Roy Fuller, whose *Collected
Poems* were published in 1962 and whose celebrated assertion that 'Poets
should be intelligible' would place him in the centre of Hough's argu-
ment; above all, it would include poets of the Movement such as Davie,
Gunn and Larkin. Nevertheless, Hough admits that 'most of the heavy
traffic' has used the 'detour'. And of course he is right. The collected
editions of largely traditional poets such as Auden and Fuller will not, at
least for the present, outweigh those of Eliot and Pound.

There can be little doubt that, during the fifties and sixties, poetry
written in English, but more especially poetry written in England, to a
large extent 'rejoined the main highway'. But how accurate is Hough's
description of that highway, and are the Movement poets really among its
travellers? Certainly, his statement that 'a poem, internally considered,
ought to make the same kind of sense as any other discourse' is very close
to Davie in *Articulate Energy* and to Robert Conquest in the intro-
duction to *New Lines* ('. . . we see refusal to abandon a rational structure
and comprehensible language, even when the verse is most highly
charged with sensuous or emotional intent' [*New Lines,* 1956, p. xv]).
That sort of clarity is one of the genuinely unifying features of the Move-
ment. But the following passage poses other problems:

> I believe that a poet's traditional quality, though it may be displayed
> and expounded by historical scholarship, actually realises itself in his
> relation to his readers, and in his relation to a certain community of
> human feeling — what Johnson called the 'uniformity of sentiment'
> that underwrites poetic communication. The traditional poet, or any
> poet so far as he is traditional, addresses his readers in the confidence
> that he will be understood; that his rhetoric and his mode of address
> will be familiar to them from their previous reading of poetry; and he
> appeals to an order of feeling that he assumes to be common to himself
> and them, simply as human beings, or as members of a particular
> civilisation.   (p. 40)

Whether the Movement poets address the Johnsonian 'common reader'
has often been questioned. In an article on Davie in 1962, Bernard
Bergonzi commented: 'a recent reviewer has remarked that the names of
over thirty writers are mentioned in *Brides of Reason.* A rapid check of my
own suggests that the number is in fact nearly forty; and this can surely be
described as hammering home a point, valid in itself, with somewhat

insolent emphasis' *(Critical Quarterly,* IV, 4, winter 1962, p. 294). And Bergonzi hammers his point home too, clearly aware that, as university teacher and literary critic, he is typical of the informed, professionally involved audience which reads contemporary poetry. Michael Hamburger echoes the same sort of concern, in a rather different tone, when he complains of verse being turned into 'a by-product of literary criticism, full of literary allusions and — what is much worse — of a piddling wit, a trivial ingenuity that cries out for the applause of learned colleagues . . .' *(Children of Albion,* 1969, p. 317). 'Where is contemporary poetry read, and where is it written?' asks Hough. 'In the universities.' This is true; and it is more true of the Movement poets than of the modernists who, in Hough's view, started the trouble. The connections between the modernists and the academic world were relatively unstable: Eliot, Pound and Williams did not make their lifelong careers in universities. Davie and Gunn, on the other hand, teach at universities (so do John Holloway and John Wain, and Kingsley Amis has been a university lecturer); Larkin is a university librarian; and one of the predominant stock responses to the Movement has been to describe it, in some vaguely unflattering way, as 'academic'. These facts suggest that this kind of postwar poetry is likely to be even more remote from the 'common reader' than modernist poetry. But this is simply not so.

Let us consider two examples of modernist poetry. For convenience, let us take first Eliot's 'A Cooking Egg',[3] which is discussed by Hough (pp. 43-4). It is a well-known poem: well-known to be baffling rather than anything much else. Hough refers us to the symposium conducted on this poem in *Essays in Criticism* (III, 3, July 1953, pp. 345-57) and directs us to C. S. Lewis's comments on it: 'we find seven adults (two of them Cambridge men) whose lives have been specially devoted to the study of poetry discussing a very short poem which has been before the world for thirty-odd years; and there is not the slightest agreement among them as to what, in any sense of the word, it means' *(De Descriptione Temporum,* 1955, p. 14; quoted by Hough, *op. cit.,* p. 43). There is little I want to add to the remarks of Hough and Lewis, but that little is rather important to my argument. Hough invites us to consider 'A Cooking Egg' as an example of a non-traditional—which is to say incomprehensible—poem; and so it is. But it is traditional in at least one fundamental respect: it follows an immediately recognisable pattern of metre and rhyme, and contains a repeated phrase ('I shall not want . . .') which is reminiscent mainly of a children's song or hymn. Admittedly, it uses these devices very selfconsciously. Still, the fact that it uses them at all distinguishes it from much of Eliot and most of Pound; and this fact indicates that the 'common reader' will be faced with a problem which is *not* typical of most modernist poetry. The problem which 'A Cooking Egg' presents is one of discrepancy between a traditional prosody and an outrageously esoteric

content. The syntax is quite straightforward: there are no especially
complex sentences; the longest sentence in the poem is five lines; the
punctuation is orthodox. But what the words add up to is another matter.
  Consider, on the other hand, the conclusion of 'The Fire Sermon' from
The Waste Land:

> 'On Margate Sands.   300
> I can connect
> Nothing with nothing.
> The broken fingernails of dirty hands.
> My people humble people who expect
> Nothing.'
>   la la
>
>
> To Carthage then I came
> Burning burning burning burning
> O Lord Thou pluckest me out
> O Lord Thou pluckest   310
>
>   burning

There is only one grammatically conventional sentence here, and that is
in lines 301-2, and it has no common-sense meaning. There is no clear
metrical unity, though there are snatches of traditional metres. The
'common reader' might justifiably say—what he could hardly say about
'A Cooking Egg'—that this doesn't even look like a poem.
  The point I want to establish here is this. There are two quite distinct
problems facing the reader of modernist poetry. The first is to discover
the sense of a poem which may appear to be meaningless or incompre-
hensible; the second is to discover why a poem which does not adhere to
accepted prosody or ordinary syntax should be treated as a poem at all.
  The first problem is not peculiar to modernist poetry, though it may be
accentuated in it. It can arise whenever the author has read more widely
or esoterically than his reader or where the author's diction is radically
different from his reader's. This is a problem of comprehension and
interpretation. The second problem is specifically concerned with
modernism. The significance of Milton's Satan has been a subject of
disagreement among readers for three hundred years, a subject to which
C. S. Lewis devoted a great deal of time; the disagreements over the
meaning of 'A Cooking Egg' which so irritated Lewis, are an extreme
form of the same debate. But everyone agrees that *Paradise Lost* is written
in sentences and in verse (and so is 'A Cooking Egg'); whereas *The Waste
Land* often isn't. When a reader understands the syntax and prosody of a
poem but not its sense he may at least retire to a library and try to work it
out; but if he cannot begin to recognise the poem's structure he is faced
with a different and perhaps insurmountable obstacle.

The question of difficulty in modernist poetry, then, is primarily related to structure rather than meaning. This sounds like the tired and familiar distinction between form and content. But by 'structure' I mean something more general than what is usually understood by 'form': I mean the element of organisation which turns a collection of words into an intelligible means of communication. And here I return to Hough's remark that 'A poem, internally considered, ought to make the same kind of sense as any other discourse.' The complexity of the discourse is not, at this point, the question at issue: the lucidity of it is. And the word 'discourse' takes on a particular resonance when we are dealing with postwar English poetry.

A fragment of weak flesh that circles round
Between the sky and the hot crust of hell,
I circle because I have found
That tracing circles is a useful spell
Against contentment, which comes on by stealth;
Because I have found that from the heaven sun
Can scorch like hell itself,
I end my circle where I had begun.

(Thom Gunn, 'A Plan of Self Subjection', *The Sense of Movement*, 1957, p. 20.)

The poem of which this is the opening stanza is discursive in a very obvious sense. It pursues an argument rather than describing a scene or an event; it relies more upon intellect than upon elegance. John Press notes, 'the close texture of the verse, its concentrated intellectual passion, and the fidelity with which the rhythmical pauses and stresses mirror the fluctuating moods of the emotional argument, are strongly reminiscent of Donne' (*Rule and Energy*, 1963, p. 195). And not only Donne: one might add that it is also reminiscent of other sixteenth- and early seventeenth-century poets; and that this places it, in the view of a critic such as Yvor Winters, in the main tradition of English poetry.

But perhaps Hough would not agree. His list of 'main highway' poets does not really allow for that kind of traditionalism or that kind of discourse. He quotes an interesting but slight lyric by Robert Frost ("To Earthward') with the declaration, 'This is a traditional poem' (p.41). Now the Frost poem certainly depends upon pre-modernist techniques. It is a good Georgian poem; it has a great deal of lyric grace; it is carefully constructed; it is effectively evocative. But I would not want to base a definition of the English poetic tradition upon it, nor can I see a view of the tradition centred upon Frost's lyricism easily embracing the abstract discourse of Gunn.

I have already suggested that Hough fails to define the problems of modernism satisfactorily, that he does not adequately distinguish between difficulty of sense and difficulty of structure. I want to suggest that his notion of traditionalism is equally faulty: for his list of traditional twentieth-century poets is really only viable if one assumes that the tradition started around the late eighteenth century, and this is a somewhat limiting view. Then there is the problem of Johnson's 'common reader' who so persistently lurks behind Hough's essay. And there is this passage:

> Deep in the folk memory of English literary critics is the echo of a time when it was possible to speak of something called 'the English spirit'. Few, in a state of full vigilance, would allow this faded trope to escape their lips now. But I intend to employ it, not meaning whatever Sir Arthur Quiller-Couch would have meant by it, but meaning something like the spirit of the language, the whole drift and pressure given by the whole body of poetry written in English. The suggestion that knocks on the door is that specifically 'modern' poetry is hostile to this spirit and has tried to move against that pressure.   (pp. 7-8)

This is almost persuasive. It is certainly true, as Charles Tomlinson and others have pointed out, that the original major forces in modern poetry in English were 'two Americans and an Irishman', and it is true too that modernism has been far less readily assimilated in England than in the USA. Nevertheless, I am not sure that Hough convincingly separates his 'English spirit' from Quiller-Couch's. He seems to recommend an unstrenuous lyric tradition, comprehensible to the 'common reader', and embodying whatever is meant by the 'English spirit'. We find exactly similar ideas of the tradition in a review of books by William Watson, Alfred Noyes and Henry Newbolt, published in 1909:

> The three poets whose names are here joined, different as they are from each other, are alike in this, that they all belong to the centre of poetic tradition. Neither [sic] of them insists on any new formula for the definition of poetry. The compass of the old instrument is, in their view, still wide enough to contain modern music. They aim at a quality of beauty in expression which demands no violent readjustment of sympathy or taste on the part of the reader. (*Times Literary Supplement*, 18 November 1909, quoted by C. K. Stead, *The New Poetic*, 1964, p. 55.)

I am not saying that Hough or anyone else wants to return to 1909; yet the literary situation then fulfilled his criteria more completely than anything since. With the decline of conservative public poets like Watson, Newbolt, Austin and Noyes, poetry lost an audience which was not professionally concerned with literature, and this audience has not— except through public readings and, in another way, through the work of John Betjeman—been regained. This question of audience needs to be handled carefully. Hough, as we have seen, is bothered by it; and C. K. Stead, in his interesting chapter '1909-16: Poets and Their Public', shows how much the innovations in poetic practice during these years depended upon dissatisfaction or anger with the predominant audience. Stead implies that the failure of the Georgian movement to provide the necessary rebellion against technical incompetence and intellectual sluggishness was due largely to their hesitancy in accepting the fact that poetry is not 'popular', and he quotes an amazingly confused statement by Harold Monro on the subject. But Eliot's position was unequivocal. In 1919, echoing—and mimicking—Yeats's 'The Fisherman', he wrote, 'It is wrong for Mr Kipling to address a large audience, but it is a better thing than to address a small one. The only better thing is to address the one hypothetical Intelligent Man who does not exist and who is the audience of the artist' (*The Athenaeum*, 9 May 1919, quoted by Stead, *op. cit.*, p. 109). It is hardly surprising, then, that modernism should appear 'hostile' to the 'English spirit'; the question is whether that spirit, the spirit of 1909, was worth preserving. And the answer is clearly no. Admirable though Hough's concern with the audience may seem, it has very little to do with literary criticism, and indeed it confuses his critical standards: discontent with the audience may act as a catalyst in a literary revolution, and there is plenty of evidence to suggest that this happened in the case of modernism; but a complacent unprofessional audience is only likely to encourage—if it encourages anything at all—complacent unprofessional poetry.

So we may dispose of the 'English spirit' and the 'common reader': not because these concepts are inherently invalid, but because, useful as they might be in a historical or sociological inquiry, they do not affect the qualitative judgement of literature except in a distracting and unhelpful way. It is surprising that Hough raises them at all, for near the beginning of *Image and Experience* he writes: 'unless we are looking at literature as a symptom of something else (a possibly respectable occupation, but not that of the literary critic), what must be attended to is the behaviour of literature itself' (p. 4). There remains the question of lyricism and discourse, and on this question Hough is not at all clear. Of course Frost's 'To Earthward' makes 'the same kind of sense as any other discourse' if this means that it is constructed of sentences which are syntactically correct in themselves and which relate to each other in a recognisable manner. This is also true of 'A Plan of Self Subjection'. And it would be true of 'A Cooking Egg' if only we could penetrate the poem's self-referential world. So as a means of distinguishing between Hough's examples it is not much use.

We are left with lyricism. 'To Earthward' is a poem which might ordinarily be described as lyrical in tone (I am not using the word 'lyric' as a synonym for 'short poem'); equally, 'A Cooking Egg' is plainly not lyrical in this sense. This is what Hough's distinction amounts to; and his own poems—in *Legends and Pastorals*, for example—are 'lyrical' in precisely this way. The word describes Frost's poetic tone and Hough's, and it has a certain application to the poetry of the last hundred and fifty years or so. But it does not describe the English poetic tradition.

To begin to discuss this tradition, we need to look closely at issues which Hough scarcely touches upon. We need to examine the continuity of syntax and of prosody; and the intellectual tradition which is more concerned with reason than with romantic lyricism: and we will find these questions dealt with in the critical work of Donald Davie and Yvor Winters.

2

Donald Davie's connections with the Movement, as poet and critic, are much closer than Hough's: 'I like to think that if the group of us had ever cohered enough to subscribe to a common manifesto, it might have been *Purity of Diction in English Verse*', he wrote in the 1966 'Postscript' to that book.[4] Both *Purity of Diction* and *Articulate Energy*, in many ways its sequel, deal with the question of modernism and its relationship with the tradition; and to this question I now return.

I have complained that Hough's distinction between modernism and traditionalism pays insufficient attention to the structural difficulty of modernist poetry. Davie, on the other hand, is specifically concerned with syntax.

> *What is common to all modern poetry is the assertion or the assumption (most often the latter) that syntax in poetry is wholly different from syntax as understood by logicians and grammarians.* When the poet retains syntactical forms acceptable to the grammarian, this is merely a convention which he chooses to observe.
>
> (*Articulate Energy*, 1955, p. 148.)

This is more promising: of the two examples from Eliot discussed above, the end of 'The Fire Sermon' bears out Davie's first contention clearly enough, while in 'A Cooking Egg' we may assume that Eliot opts for a traditional prosodic and syntactical structure to produce just the effect of discrepancy already noted. But when Davie comes to compare a specific traditional poem with a specific modernist one, his examples—Wordsworth's 'Stepping Westward' and Pound's 'The Gypsy'—are really no better than Hough's. Davie says that 'Pound's is a musical syntax, where Wordsworth's is not' (p. 156), and this in itself is true: but syntax as music does not necessarily exclude what we might almost call 'syntax' as syntax — that is, the ordinary dictionary sense, 'the grammatical arrangement of words in speech or writing', the syntax of the grammarian. (One might add that Langland's is a musical syntax, and so is Campion's.)

Of course Davie realises this. Early in *Articulate Energy* he writes:

But it is more important to realise that syntax may have gone from a poem even when all the syntactical forms in the poem are perfect and correct . . . There is no harm in syntactical forms, so long as their function is perverted, so long as they are emptied of the significance they have in scientific explanation. It might seem, for instance, that syntax goes out of a poem along with punctuation; for (to take it on the most elementary level) the different lengths of pause signified by comma, colon, and full-stop are invaluable aids to the control of rhythm. Hence the poet may construct a complex sentence, not because the terms in the sentence are to be articulated subtly and closely, but just because he wants at that point a rhythmical unit unusually elaborate ånd sustained. In this case, articulation is by rhythm, and syntax only *seems* to be doing the articulating; it is pseudo-syntax, a play of empty forms. (pp. 9-10)

There is an air of 'hot ice and wondrous strange snow' about all this: 'syntax may have gone from the poem even when all the syntactical forms are perfect and correct'? Something is wrong here. Either this is non-sense or else the terminology is inadequate, in which case a paraphrase might help: perhaps 'logical construction may have gone from a poem . . .'? But 'logical construction' is not precisely what we understand by syntax: it introduces the notion of the meaning of words, the sense words make (which implies that 'A Cooking Egg', in which the words appear to make very little sense, is unsyntactical). Davie acknowledges elsewhere in *Articulate Energy* that the grammarian and the logician may understand different things by 'syntax', and what he surely means is that the logician's syntax may have gone while the grammarian's remains. To this we can agree, while noting that the opposite may be true, as in this stanza from a poem by Elaine Feinstein:

and yet we go towards birthdays and other
marks   not wryly   not thriftily
waiting, for where shall we find it, a
joyous, a various world? in a fury
we share, which keeps us, without
resignation: tender whenever we touch   what
else we share   this flesh   we
bring together   it hurts to
think of dying as we lie close

('Marriage', *The Magic Apple Tree,* 1971, p. 58.)

The last, completely unpunctuated part of this stanza could be arranged as logical syntactical prose without much difficulty; and in the process a grammatical order would be imposed upon it. The result would be different grammatically; it would be impoverished musically; but logically it would be precisely the same. So, when Davie writes, 'It might seem, for instance, that syntax goes out of a poem along with punctuation; but this is not the case', we can take it that he again means the syntax of the logician: for the grammarian's syntax must disappear, or be obscured, when punctuation, which is its chief means of expression, is removed. In Mrs Feinstein's excellent poem, the logic, the music and the rhythm successfully articulate what is usually done by grammatical syntax: there is no loss of clarity. But this is rare: the predominant fault of poetry which abandons grammatical syntax is not so much the tendency for music to take over the function of articulation as the tendency for the music itself, overburdened, to degenerate into cacophony.

And what of 'pseudo-syntax'? Can there be such a thing? According to the logician there can: for the logician will appeal to the 'function' of syntactical forms, 'the significance they have in scientific explanation'. The grammarian on the other hand might reply more modestly that the use to which syntactical forms are put is not his business. His modesty would be prudent, because the logician is heading for a muddle. 'In this case, articulation is by rhythm, and syntax only *seems* to be doing the articulating; it is a pseudo-syntax, a play of empty forms.' One may object first of all that articulation is always by rhythm: the syntactical structure of a sentence, in verse or in prose, imposes a rhythmical structure. Davie has already said that 'the different lengths of pauses signified by comma, colon, and full-stop are invaluable aids to the control of rhythm.' So they are: Mrs Feinstein risks a great deal when she does without them. Grammatical syntax and rhythm can be made to work against each other by juxtaposition, and every line of poetry which ends in mid-phrase (or, for that matter, in mid-word) does just this; but such juxtaposition is in itself a kind of merging, and is pointless unless we are aware that two intertwined syntactical structures—the grammatical and the rhythmical—are being presented. And 'empty forms'? The notion is rather ludicrous, suggesting an unstarted crossword puzzle or a sentence in which the words are represented by empty square brackets. The logician contends that a syntactical form is empty if it does not make logical sense; the grammarian contends that a 'perfect and correct' syntactical form cannot be empty—it contains an acceptable grammatical organisation of words, and that is enough.

No doubt much of what I have just said about this passage of Davie's will seem obtuse, so I must add that this obtuseness is meant to serve a purpose. For what we have discovered in this passage is a disagreement between the grammarian and the logician which cannot end amicably because neither really knows what the other is talking about. If we are to talk about syntax with any degree of clarity, we shall have to take sides: and it will be clear by now that I have sided with the grammarian. The grammarian will not, I think, be outraged or perplexed by Pound's 'The Gypsy'; but the logician will be baffled:

For consider: who is 'up on the wet road near Clermont'? The authentic Romanies? Or the half-castes with whom they must not be confused? Or the poet himself, and the man he has encountered? We do not know, and it does not matter.   *(Articulate Energy*, p. 156.) Precisely: it does not matter. It does not matter because the grammatical syntax is correct (and elegant); consequently we are faced with a stylish and deliberate ambiguity. The syntax is very carefully telling us nothing, or rather suggesting a number of things simultaneously. The logician is offended: what of the 'function' of syntactical forms, 'the significance they have in scientific explanation'? To which the grammarian may reply: perhaps syntactical forms can have more than one function. (And to which the poet may reply that scientific explanation does not necessarily interest him.)

Of course, the grammarian will have no difficulty in finding passages in Pound which will offend him.

It was Saturday the 1st day of April, toward noon,
the Senate not being that day in session . . .
    came to my room at Brown's asking was I
Mrs Clay's blood-relation?
Prompt in agreeing to meet . . . exact in protesting Clay's
    right to call him. 'Col. Tatnall, the bearer,
    is authorized . . . .'
Was defiance of Adams, not Clay,
    in the senate speech, but to Jessup had said
He would waive privilege
    which constitutes a very palpable difference.

                                                ('Canto LXXXVIII')

This at least bears some approximation to syntax, and it is all in English, unlike much of the *Cantos*: the syntax has been chopped up but not entirely obliterated. Nevertheless, to speak, as we did when dealing with 'The Gypsy', of 'ambiguity' would be plainly absurd: this is chaos, not ambiguity. And it is chaos because whereas 'The Gypsy' presents a calculated loss of clarity within a recognisable structure, 'Canto LXXX-VIII' confuses the structure itself. It is an expertly wrought kind of chaos, certainly, and these objections to it are merely those of the grammarian. But the grammarian's disapproval may at least indicate that this is a peculiarly modernist poem in structural terms, while 'The Gypsy' isn't.

Pound himself has, as one would expect, formulated the problem concisely:

A people that grows accustomed to sloppy writing is a people in the process of losing grip on its empire and on itself. And this looseness and blowsiness is not anything as simple and scandalous as abrupt and disordered syntax.

It concerns the relation of expression to meaning. Abrupt and dis-ordered syntax can be at times very honest, and an elaborately

constructed sentence can be at times merely an elaborate camouflage.
(*ABC of Reading*, 1934, p. 86; quoted by Davie,
Purity of Diction in English Verse, 1967, p. 93.)

Now it seems to me that the 'looseness and blowsiness' to which Pound
refers may be brought about by the disintegration of logical syntax; while
the 'abrupt and disordered syntax' which 'can be at times very honest' is
none other than the fragmented grammatical syntax which I take to be an
important characteristic of modernist poetry. It can, certainly, 'be at
times very honest', though whether that kind of honesty is an adequate
end for poetry is another matter. 'Beauty is, or it includes, order; ugliness
is or includes muddle', says Davie (*Articulate Energy*, p. 145), thereby
denying the possibility that Pound's disordered but honest syntax might
be beautiful. And yet 'beautiful' is just the sort of word we might use, in a
slack way, about the *Cantos*: we might use the word as a last resort and say
that the *Cantos* are disordered, incoherent, pretentious, but beautiful; or
(to anticipate a little) we might agree with Yvor Winters when he writes of
Canto IV, 'The loveliness of such poetry appears to me indubitable, but it
is merely a blur of revery' (*In Defense of Reason*, 1949, p. 59)—which is a
better way of saying much the same thing. On the surface, there seems to
be an absolute opposition between Pound's statement and Davie's; then
we return to the first passage from Davie quoted in this section. It looks
like a useful clarifying statement, and Davie's italics proclaim that this is
what it is meant to be. But it really adds to the confusion by adding a third
variety of syntax (modernist) to the other two. Of course Davie is right to
point out that 'Mallarmé and Valéry, when they speak of "syntax", do not
mean by it what is meant by the common reader' (*Articulate Energy*, p.
149); but Pound, in the passage quoted above, means just the same thing
as the common reader. So to introduce the idea of 'modernist syntax' is
misleading if only because one of modernism's main architects uses the
word 'syntax' in a traditional way. We must conclude that a syntactically
traditional poem is one which conforms to the grammarian's principles of
organisation and a syntactically modernist poem is one which offends
against them.

3

In the first two sections of this chapter I have been concerned with
defining (or, depending on one's viewpoint, quibbling about) certain
words: modernism, traditionalism, structure, syntax. And I have dealt in
some detail with specific passages from two contemporary critics. In spite
of their differences, Hough and Davie would share certain widely held
assumptions about English poetry: for example, that Wordsworth is a
major traditional poet, or that Pound is a major modernist one. I shall
now turn to a critic who disagrees entirely with the first of these assump-

tions and who has considerable reservations about the second.

Yvor Winters was not afraid of generalisations:

The two great periods in the poetry of our language are the period from Wyatt to Dryden, inclusive, and the period from Jones Very to the present, and the second period does not seem to have come to an end. In the second period there are only a few poets from the British Isles of any importance: Hardy, Bridges, T. Sturge Moore in particular; and, in their various ways, Hopkins, Yeats, Elizabeth Daryush, and Thom Gunn. The rest are American, and many of the Americans are very great, and there are among the Americans some minor poets as distinguished as the best of the Renaissance. (*Forms of Discovery*, 1967, p. 358).

Two things need to be said at the outset about this deliberately provocative statement. The first is that few people read Sturge Moore, until recently few had read Mrs Daryush, and few have heard of Jones Very: they are listed at least partly to emphasise omissions. The second is that in discarding writers of the Romantic period Winters discards a great deal of what is usually meant by the English poetic tradition. Wordsworth, says Winters (expressing an opinion shared by Pound), 'is a very bad poet who nevertheless wrote a few good lines.'

Let us consider 'Composed upon Westminster Bridge'. The opening line is an example of one of the worst formulae of amateur writing: 'Earth has not anything to show more fair'. The line says nothing about the scene. 'She is the most beautiful woman I have ever seen.' 'What a glorious day!' This is the ultimate in stylistic indolence. The next three and two-thirds lines proceed in much the same way. Then to the end of the octet we have simple but excellent description. The next three lines revert to the formula of the opening, and the twelfth line states a ridiculous falsehood in the interests of romantic pomposity: the river does not glide at its own sweet will, and this is very fortunate for London; the river glides according to the law of gravitation, and a much better line could have been made of this fact. Of the last two lines, the houses are good, the two exclamations mere noise.

(*Forms of Discovery*, pp. 167-8.)

In an obvious sense, this is not especially good criticism. The joke about London is too smug; the concession to the houses of line 13 is patronising. But this is Winters's characteristic negative tone (by which I mean not that he is always negative, but that his tone and method when dealing with poems he likes are rather different). And if the method here is disconcerting, the judgement is surely right. 'Composed upon Westminster Bridge' is not a very good poem. Probably we know this already: Wordsworth's reputation is less inflated than it used to be. The reputation of Yeats, on the other hand, shows few signs of declining. Here is Winters on the final stanza of 'Among School Children':

The term *labour* seems to mean fruitful labor or ideal labor, and a labor which costs no effort. But where does this kind of labor exist, except, perhaps, in the life of a tree? The body is always bruised to pleasure soul: wisdom is always born out of midnight oil or out of something comparable. The diction in these lines is abominable: the first two lines are bad enough, but the third and fourth are as bad as Keats's 'Here where men sit and hear each other groan.' The question addressed to the tree is preposterous: the tree is obviously more than the leaf, the blossom or the bole, but these all exist and can be discussed, and it is because of this fact that we have words for them— the implication of the passage is that the tree is an inscrutable unit, like the Mallarméan poem. The diction of the seventh line is as bad as that of the third and fourth. The last line is similar to the fifth and sixth. When we watch the dancer we may not discriminate, although a choreographer could; but if the dancer and the dance could not be discriminated in fact, the dancer could never have learned the dance. Precisely the same ideas will be found in Emerson's 'Blight', a small affair but somewhat better written.

(Forms of Discovery, p. 220.)

This quotation comes from a fairly extensive essay on Yeats, much of which is a good deal less hostile than this passage. I have quoted at length to illustrate Winters's procedure: his admirable terseness; his careful line-by-line analysis; his obsession with accuracy. And the passage also indicates some of his characteristic flaws: he tends seriously to undervalue previously overrated writers just because of their reputation; while deflating Yeatsian rhetoric, he employs his own rhetoric rather carelessly—words like 'abominable' and 'preposterous' turn up too often; and he has a habit of forcing wry jokes, which can be funny in themselves, to play too crucial a part in his argument. Despite these faults, and some of them are serious, it should be clear that Winters's dislike of romantic poetry is not merely eccentric; on the contrary, it is carefully reasoned, and 'reason' is a key word in his critical theory.

It is precisely this emphasis on reason which permits Winters to make (admittedly at the expense of Wordsworth and Yeats, among others) a sensible and coherent distinction between traditional and modernist poetry where Hough and Davie fail to do so. In his earliest major critical work, *Primitivism and Decadence,* he comments as follows on a stanza from Eliot's 'Burbank with a Baedeker; Bleistein with a Cigar':

Burbank crossed a little bridge,
   Descending at a small hotel;
Princess Volupine arrived,
   They were together, and he fell.

What is the significance of the facts in the first two lines? They have no real value as perception: the notation is too perfunctory. They must have some value as information, as such details might have value, for example, in a detective story, if they are to have any value at all. Yet they have no bearing on what follows; in fact, most of what follows is obscure in exactly the same way. They are not even necessary to what occurs in the next two lines, for Princess Volupine might just as well have encountered him anywhere else and after any other transit.

(In Defense of Reason, p. 47.)

Now this obviously has some bearing on the earlier problem of 'A Cooking Egg', where the obscurity is of the same kind (the information appears to be valueless) though several degrees more dense. And in both poems the obscurity is additionally infuriating since it is couched in a simple, not to say simple-minded, prosodic structure. Davie would call this 'pseudo-syntax'; Winters's description of it as 'pseudo-reference' is more helpful because it creates no problems of terminology: and although Winters places his comments on Pound's *Cantos* in *Primitivism and Decadence* under a different heading ('Qualitative Progression'), the connection between these comments and the remarks on Eliot quoted above is abundantly clear. Winters writes of Canto IV:

The loveliness of such poetry appears to me indubitable, but it is merely a blur of revery: its tenuity becomes apparent if one compares it, for example, to the poetry of Paul Valéry, which achieves effects of imagery, particularly of atmospheric imagery, quite as extraordinary, along with precision, depth of meaning, and the power that comes of close and inalterable organisation, and, though Mr Pound's admirers have given him a great name as a metrist, with incomparably finer effects of sound.

(In Defense of Reason, p. 59.)

Once again, Winters's primary objection is that the information is not sufficiently meaningful: Pound, he says, 'resembles a village loafer who sees much and understands little' *(ibid.,* p. 58). It is worth noting the qualities he especially admires in Valéry: precision; depth of meaning; close and inalterable organisation; finer effects of sound. Almost any reader would agree that these are among the qualities one finds in great poetry: yet Winters does not find them, or enough of them, in Wordsworth, Yeats, Eliot or Pound.

(Winters's attitude to Pound shifted slightly between the publication of *Primitivism and Decadence* in 1937 and his last book [excluding the posthumous *Uncollected Essays and Reviews*], *Forms of Discovery,* in 1967. In the latter book he writes of Canto IV: 'The detail in this Canto is remarkable throughout, but is heavily inlaid with poetical mannerism.' And a little later: 'the details and cadences in the early *Cantos* are very lovely . . .' Yet: 'it is not great poetry; it is superior Swinburne' [*Forms of Discovery,* p. 317].)

The most concise statement of Winters's notion of the major English

poetic tradition is not to be found in his criticism but in one of his poems,
'Time and the Garden':

> These trees, whose slow growth measures off my years,
> I would expand to greatness. No one hears,
> And I am still retarded in duress!
> And this is like that other restlessness
> To seize the greatness not yet fairly earned,
> One which the tougher poets have discerned—
> Gascoigne, Ben Jonson, Greville, Raleigh, Donne,
> Poets who wrote great poems, one by one,
> And spaced by many years, each line an act
> Through which few labor, which no men retract.

(Collected Poems, 1952, p. 120.)

The poets cited here are among those dealt with in Winters's most
influential critical essay, 'The Sixteenth-century Lyric in England: A
Critical and Historical Reinterpretation'. This essay is by now well-
known, both in its original and revised versions,[5] and many of its
perceptions have passed into general academic currency, often without
acknowledgement. In it, Winters defines the two schools of Elizabethan
poetry and presents reading-lists of the 'best poems' of Googe, Turber-
ville, Gascoigne, Wyatt, Sidney, Greville, Jonson and others. And he
insists that the poems be read, for the essay is quite meaningless other-
wise. In the present context, however, what is especially significant is the
connection between the poetry of the sixteenth-century 'plain style' and
that of our own time.

This connection is most forcefully stated by Winters in his essay on J. V.
Cunningham, whom he considered 'the most consistently distinguished
poet writing in English today, and one of the finest in the language'
(Forms of Discovery, p. 299); and this essay forms the major part of the
chapter 'The Plain Style Reborn' in Forms of Discovery. He has this to say
of Cunningham's style:

> The mature style is what we would call the plain style if we met it in the
> Renaissance. It is free of ornament, almost without sensory detail, and
> compact. But it is a highly sophisticated version of the plain style, and
> is very complex without loss of clarity. It comes closer, perhaps, to Ben
> Jonson and a few of his immediate contemporaries than to anyone
> else.

(Forms of Discovery, p. 308.)

This is an accurate description, and it is reinforced by the mastery of the
epigram which Cunningham shares with Jonson. Clearly, too,
Cunningham's virtues are also to be found (though not, in Winters's
opinion, to the same degree) in other contemporary poets: in certain
poems of Auden and of Empson; in several poems by Winters himself
and by other poets associated with the American publisher Alan

Swallow; and, perhaps above all, in the best work of the outstanding Movement poets, Donald Davie and Thom Gunn. Gunn's poem 'A Mirror for Poets' emphasises the part played by Elizabethan England as a continuing background to his work; and his later poem, 'To Yvor Winters, 1955', not only reiterates some of Winters's criteria but also catches something of his tone:

> But sitting in the dusk—though shapes combine,
> Vague mass replacing edge and flickering line,
> You keep both Rule and Energy in view,
> Much power in each, most in the balanced two:
> Ferocity existing in the fence
> Built by an exercised intelligence.
> Though night is always near, complete negation
> Ready to drop on wisdom and emotion,
> Night from the air or the carnivorous breath,
> Still it is right to know the force of death,
> And, as you do, persistent, tough in will,
> Raise from the excellent the better still.
>
> *(The Sense of Movement,* p. 44.)

The balance of Rule and Energy offers itself as an almost plausible formula for defining traditional poetry: in an obvious sense, modernist writing tends to achieve Energy at the expense of Rule. Yet it will not quite do. Ultimately when we come to define the main tradition of English poetry we must find ourselves talking, with Winters, about the 'plain style'; or, with Davie, about economy of metaphor and 'purity of diction'; or even, with Hough, about that 'English spirit', dubious as the expression may be, to which modernism is hostile: and we will realize that, if each of them is not quite speaking of the same thing, there is nevertheless a common impetus at work. Admittedly, each critic anchors his version of the tradition in a different place, and these places seem to be mutually incompatible: but all three are engaged in a quest for clarity, and clarity has not been a conspicuous feature of modernist theory or practice. The quests lead in different directions: thus, Hough's clarity is largely a matter of tone, to be found in the conventional lyric poem; Davie's a matter of syntax and economy, to be found in the Augustans and elsewhere; and Winters's a matter of reasoned intellect, to be found in the Renaissance and in the twentieth century. But perhaps all three would agree that much of the best poetry written in England since the Second World War conforms to their various notions of clarity and marks a return to the mainstream or, as Hough calls it, the 'main highway'. In reading it, we should seek—to borrow a distinction from Frank Kermode—continuities rather than schisms.

NOTES

1. In fact, interestingly and ironically, Hough is echoing Eliot here: 'The poet must be very conscious of the main current, which does not at all flow invariably through the most distinguished reputations.' T. S. Eliot, 'Tradition and the Individual Talent', *Selected Essays*, 1951, p. 16.

2. John Wain, 'Ambiguous Gifts', *Penguin New Writing*, 40, 1950, pp. 116-28. The title 'The Movement' was not of course invented by the poets concerned nor was it coined by Anthony Hartley (as Ian Hamilton claims in his essay (The Making of the Movement')): J. D. Scott was the author of the unsigned article ('In the Movement') published in *Spectator*, 1 October 1954, from which the term originates.

3. T. S. Eliot, *Collected Poems*, 1963, p. 46. Reviewing that edition, Donald Davie commented as follows on this particular poem: ' "A Cooking Egg", for instance, deserves nothing much better than the fate which has come upon it— of being the occasion for a protracted critical wrangle . . .' (*New Statesman*, 11 October 1963).

4. Donald Davie, *Purity of Diction in English Verse*, 1967, pp. 197-8. This is a lithographic reprint of the first edition (1952) with an additional postscript. It is worth noting that the book on its first publication was not received with unqualified enthusiasm by the poets who were to become associated with the Movement: John Wain, in a generally unfavourable review, complained, 'The trouble is that the blunders have more vitality than the sound parts' (*Mandrake*, II, 9, 1953, pp. 265-6).

5. Originally published in *Poetry* (Chicago), February, March, April 1939. Reprinted in *Elizabethan Poetry: Modern Essays in Criticism*, ed. Paul J. Alpers, 1967. A revised version of the essay appears as chapter 1 of *Forms of Discovery*.

Chapter Two

THOM GUNN: A PIERGLASS FOR POETS

1

In night when colours all to black are cast,
Distinction lost, or gone down with the light;
The eye a watch to inward senses plac'd,
Not seeing, yet still having power of sight,

Gives vain alarums to the inward sense,
Where fear stirr'd up with witty tyranny,
Confounds all powers, and thorough self-offence,
Doth forge and raise impossibility:

Such as in thick depriving darknesses,
Proper reflections of the error be,
And images of self-confusednesses,
Which hurt imaginations only see;

   And from this nothing seen, tells news of devils,
   Which but expressions be of inward evils.

This is the hundredth poem in Fulke Greville's *Caelica*, quoted from the edition edited by Thom Gunn in 1968 (p. 129). One hardly need remark that it is an extraordinary poem: at once complex and compact, intellectually intense, and perfectly wrought—the kind of poem which both invites and deserves a long and intricate analysis. My purpose here is simply to point out a few features of the poem which may illuminate Gunn's interest in Greville and at the same time indicate possible approaches to Gunn's own poetry.

The poem defines clarity by describing the workings of confusion. The passive verb in the very first line gives an initial clue to its method: who or what casts colours 'all to black'? In the second line, the word 'or' shows that the process of confusion has begun already: *because* distinction is lost, it is impossible to decide whether it is in fact lost or merely 'gone down with the light'. The eye is diverted from its customary function, which is surely to observe outward, and forced instead to look inward: but we know from the first two lines that the faculty of sight will be unable to cope with the inward confusion. The rational process short-circuits: the eye can give only 'vain alarums' to the 'inward sense' which is in any case the object of the primary confusion; and the mind, incapable of acting as a controlling force except in conjunction with the power of sight, becomes a 'witty tyranny'. The 'self-offence' of line 7 is the distortion caused by the denial of the rational self which exists in light and, as Gunn rightly notes, in nature.

In the sestet, the poem moves from the effects of ordinary darkness to the 'thick depriving darknesses' of Hell itself (and the verse alters accordingly: 'darknesses'/'confusednesses' must be one of the most menacing rhymes in the language). Simultaneously, the language becomes more explicitly moral: words like 'proper', 'error', 'hurt', 'devils', 'evils' on the one hand reinforce our awareness that this is a religious poem dealing with the religious Hell and on the other remind us that it is a poem about ideas and abstractions in the broadest sense. The final couplet purports to lower the tension, but one is left with the suspicion that the 'inward evils' are no less powerful than the devils by which they are represented.

This sonnet is an example of what Yvor Winters calls the Elizabethan 'plain style' at its most concise; and it is not hard to discover at least some of its virtues in the poetry of Thom Gunn. Gunn has so far published seven full-length books of verse. The poems I shall discuss in the first section of this chapter come from his first collection, *Fighting Terms* (the book has been substantially revised on two occasions, and I shall refer mainly to the 1962 Faber text).

The poems in *Fighting Terms* were written while Gunn was an undergraduate, which does not so much excuse the book's flaws as make them necessary. The brashness of a poem like 'Lofty in the Palais de Danse' is readily distinguishable from the mannerism into which it develops in *The Sense of Movement*. And, necessarily, there are a number of voices to be heard in the poems: most readers will have noticed, for instance, the presence of Yeats in 'Incident on a Journey', and there is no good reason to suppose that Gunn did not put him there deliberately; equally, as John Press has pointed out in *Rule and Energy* (p.192), 'Without a Counterpart' leans heavily on Graves' 'The Terraced Valley'; elsewhere, Auden[1] and Edwin Muir are obvious and natural influences, though the echoes of Eliot are perhaps a little more surprising. Throughout the book, Gunn seems eager to demonstrate his conversance with literature and with mythology, and the effect is sometimes over-studiously literary. At the same time, he is already more than competent at handling a wide range of technical devices which owe much to sixteenth and seventeenth century poetry: repetitions, circularities, abstractions, tight rhyme-schemes and metres. Consider 'Wind in the Street':

The same faces, and then the same scandals
Confront me inside the talking-shop which I

Frequent for my own good. And an assistant
Points to the old cogwheels, the old handles
Set in machines which to buy would be to buy
The same faces, and then the same scandals.

I climb by the same stairs to a square attic,
Where I pause, for surely this is something new!
So square, so simple. It is new to be so simple.
Then I see the same sky through the skylight, static,
Cloudless, the same artificial toy-like blue.
The same stairs led to the same attic.

I only came, I explain, to look round.
I think that I have seen this line before.
Searching thoroughly, I did not see what I wanted.
What I wanted would have been what I found.
The assistant coos, I go to the shop door:
I only came, I explain, to look round.

I may return, meanwhile I'll look elsewhere:
My want may modify to what I have seen.
I step into the street, where I regain
The struggle with an uncommitted air,
Struggle with fluency, the state between
To which I still return who look elsewhere.

                                    (*Fighting Terms*, 1962, p. 11)

One notices, first of all, the repetitions—the insistence on the word
'same', the typical Gunn construction 'which to buy would be to buy'—
and the circularity of each stanza. And these devices cause surprisingly
little strain, though the last line of the second stanza jars badly. One
notices secondly the poverty of concrete detail: even the cogwheels and
handles seem to have been borrowed from Yeats' rag-and-bone shop.
But, as in so much of Gunn's work, the concrete details are mainly a
pretext for working out abstract riddles which may also become
syntactical riddles: the concrete details fade easily into abstraction, the
attic is merely square, the sky merely static. In the second half of the
poem, we find two examples of a persistent mannerism of Gunn's, the
self-contained statement which hovers uneasily between epigram and
cracker-motto: 'What I wanted would have been what I found'; 'My want
may modify to what I have seen'. These lines, and much else in the poem,
are strikingly close to Eliot in 'Little Gidding':

    It would be the same at the end of the journey,
    If you came at night like a broken king,
    If you came by day not knowing what you came for,
    It would be the same, when you leave the rough road
    And turn behind the pig-sty to the dull façade

And the tombstone. And what you thought you came for
Is only a shell, a husk of meaning
From which the purpose breaks only when it is fulfilled
If at all. Either you had no purpose
Or the purpose is beyond the end you figured
And is altered in fulfilment.

> (T. S. Eliot, *Collected Poems 1909-1962*.
> 1963, pp. 214-5)

It is perhaps only in the last four lines of 'Wind in the Street' that one can glimpse the particular fluency with abstraction which distinguishes much of Gunn's best work (the conclusion compares interestingly with the conclusion of 'On the Move'): the phrase *'an* uncommitted air' and the syntactical inversion of the final line are especially characteristic.

'Wind in the Street' is by no means a great poem, but it is well-made and intelligent; furthermore, the method and the style are undeniably Gunn's own. This can be said of a very creditable proportion of the poems in *Fighting Terms*. The first poem in the 1962 edition of the book (though not in the earlier editions), 'The Wound', is notable for the absence of the stylistic devices which I have mentioned in discussing 'Wind in the Street' and which reappear in poems such as 'Round and Round' and 'Carnal Knowledge'. It is set in the Trojan War and owes less to Homer than to *Troilus and Cressida*, as John Fuller suggested in a review of *Fighting Terms* (*The Review*, 1, 1962, pp. 29-34; reprinted in *The Modern Poet*, ed. Ian Hamilton, 1968, pp.17-22). Fuller draws attention to the following lines:

Achilles:
I see my reputation is at stake;
My fame is shrewdly gored.
Patroclus:
>   O, then, beware!
Those wounds heal ill that men do give themselves.

> (*Troilus and Cressida*, III:3:227-9)

This is obviously relevant but unfortunately it is not very helpful. In a way, it does not greatly matter whether the wound is love, or loss of self-esteem, or some other psychological condition: Gunn very deliberately does not particularise. The poem is wonderfully confident and effective, but its surface meaning is obscure and any literal interpretation is likely to run into trouble: it really will not do to say, as Alan Bold does, that 'the poem is spoken by a wounded soldier who has fought on both sides of the Trojan war and been wounded' (Alan Bold, *Thom Gunn and Ted Hughes*, 1976, p.18). If the poem is 'spoken' by anyone at all, it is spoken by Achilles (the narrative details which appear to contradict this in the first half of the poem are part of Achilles' delirium). In this way, since the wound is the psychological condition compounded of love and grief at

Patroclus' death, the poem's conclusion becomes an explanation and an apologia for Achilles' behaviour in the last act of *Troilus and Cressida:*

I was myself: subject to no man's breath:
My own commander was my enemy.
And while my belt hung up, sword in the sheath,
Thersites shambled in and breathlessly
Cackled about my friend Patroclus' death.

I called for armour, rose, and did not reel.
But, when I thought, rage at his noble pain
Flew to my head, and turning I could feel
My wound break open wide. Over again
I had to let those storm-lit valleys heal.

(Fighting Terms, p. 9)

The final line brings in an element of typically Gunnian reflexiveness both in the verbal echo of the first line ('The huge wound in my head began to heal') and in the implication that, whenever Achilles recovers sufficiently to think rationally, he recalls Patroclus' death, and the wound reopens.

In 'The Wound' the Trojan War acts as a background to an exploration of a psychological condition; in other poems war—and specifically the notion of strategy—is used to image human relationships. Many of what one might loosely describe, with some reluctance, as Gunn's early love poems (such as 'To His Cynical Mistress', 'Carnal Knowledge', 'The Beach Head', 'Tamer and Hawk', 'Captain in Time of Peace') use, explicitly or implicitly, the language and patterns of war as metaphors for the strategies of love. This gives to Gunn's early work a curious and to some readers rebarbative moral flavour: relationships are seen in terms of manoeuvres because all actions are based upon decisions, upon existential choices. 'The Beach Head' makes this point well. The choices are set out in the fifth stanza:

Shall I be a John a Gaunt and with my band
Of mad bloods pass in one spectacular dash,
Fighting before and after, through your land,
To issue out unharmed the farther side,
With little object other than panache
And showing what great odds may be defied?

And in the seventh:

Or shall I wait and calculate my chances,
Consolidating this my inch-square base,
Picking off rival spies that tread your glances:
Then plan when you have least supplies or clothing
A pincer-move to end in an embrace,
And risk that your mild liking turn to loathing?

(Fighting Terms, p. 30)

One cannot help feeling uneasy about this poem. Part of the trouble is that Gunn pursues his chosen image, which casts an ironic glance back to Eliot's 'Prufrock', too thoroughly and mechanically: the expertise is admirable, but the resulting poem is overburdened and artificial. Nor is the language entirely satisfactory, unhappily juxtaposing military terms and emotional introspection. Despite all this, 'The Beach Head' has a formal strength and a kind of relentless logic that compel attention.

The poem based upon a strategic choice is one of Gunn's characteristic modes of dealing with human relationships; another is the exploration of a paradox in which the individuals involved exchange roles (an idea which Gunn perhaps inherited from another Tudor model, Wyatt), as in 'Tamer and Hawk'. Here, the controlling image seems less mechanical and more apt than in 'The Beach Head': partly, one suspects, because the poem itself is more compact. The opening stanza, sparse both in language and in punctuation, demonstrates Gunn's talent for powerful simplicity:

> I thought I was so tough,
> But gentled at your hands
> Cannot be quick enough
> To fly for you and show
> That when I go I go
> At your commands.

> (*Fighting Terms*, p. 33)[2]

This could hardly be improved upon. The penultimate line condenses the kind of repetition I mentioned in discussing the first stanza of 'Wind in the Street', and one feels no strain of artificial cleverness. Similarly, in the second stanza, a small but telling pun ('I am blind to other birds—/The habit of your words/Has hooded me.') works naturally and unobtrusively. Only at the conclusion does Gunn's fondness for riddling paradox nearly overbalance the poem:

> You but half-civilize,
> Taming me in this way.
> Through having only eyes
> For you I fear to lose,
> I lose to keep, and choose
> Tamer as prey.

Though this is by no means obscure, the clarity of the poem is slightly undermined: lines 3-5 seem a little over-condensed for the sake of the form, though this incidentally increases the forcefulness of the final line.

Of the 'love poems' in *Fighting Terms*, the best known is probably 'Carnal Knowledge', and it will serve to illustrate a third mode which reappears in later books. This is succinctly stated in the opening of the poem: 'Even in bed I pose' (*Fighting Terms*, p. 20). The trouble with Gunn's poses, or more precisely those with which he invests his subjects, is that one is rarely certain of their exact purpose or nature: unlike Yeats' masks, to which they clearly owe something. 'Carnal Knowledge' may be less vague in this respect than a later poem such as 'Elvis Presley', but it remains the subject of some confusion and it has provoked a certain amount of baffled commentary. John Press writes of 'the poet's virility being flaunted' (*Rule and Energy*, p. 191): yet surely the poem is more exactly about a *pose* of virility which is seen to disintegrate later on in the poem:

> I hardly hoped for happy thoughts, although
> In a most happy sleeping time I dreamt
> We did not hold each other in contempt.

And:

> Abandon me to stammering, and go. . .

Press implies that the 'contempt' is emotional rather than sexual, but there is nothing in the poem to suggest that it might not be both. Critics (and I am thinking here especially of John Fuller's piece to which I have already referred: 'Often we were aware of a division between affection and sex') have too readily assumed that Gunn's treatment of love as strategy entails an arbitrary distinction between emotional and sexual relationships. Such a distinction is not always supported by the poems themselves. I suspect the same sort of feeling as Fuller's underlies Martin Dodsworth's comments on the first stanza of the poem:

> Surely one is struck in this poem by the incongruity of the style; the situation demands a cry from the speaker, and not the deliberation of speech which Gunn supplies and which, I think, we may legitimately describe as a stifled or inhibited cry.
>
> (Martin Dodsworth, 'Thom Gunn', in
> *The Survival of Poetry*, ed. Martin
> Dodsworth, 1970, p. 210)

This is fair enough, so long as we accept, with Dodsworth, 'the total pointlessness of the attempt at "poise" in such a situation.' But I am not sure that the poem allows us to do this so easily. However, Press, Fuller and Dodsworth are all considerably less wide of the mark than the unfortunate Alan Bold who, after quoting the opening phrase, offers the peculiar comment: 'Gunn's is very much a pre-Women's Liberation view of sex' (*Thom Gunn and Ted Hughes*, p. 21). Gunn has obviously felt unhappy about the poem and has revised it extensively, eliminating in the course of his revision its original formal distinction (the refrain 'You know I know you know I know you know' alternating with 'I know you know I know you know I know'). I quote from the 1954 text the whole of the first stanza:

> Even in bed I pose: desire may grow
> More circumstantial and less circumspect
> Each night, but an acute girl would suspect
> That my self is not like my body, bare.

I wonder if you know, or, knowing, care?
You know I know you know I know you know.

(Fighting Terms, 1954, p. 9)

As in 'The Wound', Gunn forestalls a certain kind of analysis by refusing to particularise: the posture is defined only negatively. Hence: 'my self is not like my body, bare' (which becomes in the 1962 version, 'My thoughts might not be, like my body, bare'—a better line, but less to the point); and, later on, 'I am not what I seem'; 'I'm still playing the same/Comical act inside the tragic game'; 'I know of no emotion we can share'. The conclusion of the poem is certainly an admission of failure, but the exact nature of the failure is left deliberately ambiguous:

Abandon me to stammering, and go;
If you have tears, prepare to cry elsewhere—
I know of no emotion we can share,
Your intellectual protests are a bore
And even now I pose, so now go, for
I know you know.

The original pose has apparently been seen to disintegrate. But was that disintegration in fact part of the pose?

The three 'love poems' I have just discussed are all defensive. This will not seem an especially odd statement to make about the first two, but 'Carnal Knowledge' looks like an aggressive poem. As I've indicated, I don't think this is so. Gunn's early poems mostly play 'the tragic game' which is a game of surfaces: 'the calculating Cupid feigning impartial-blind' ('To His Cynical Mistress', *Fighting Terms*, p. 10) is the referee. The poems are concerned, like Wyatt's, with the creation of intellectual patterns, which often they do meticulously, and there is seldom much point in searching for Real Life in them. In their relentless abstraction and metaphysical urgency they have more in common with Wyatt and Greville than with obvious influences such as Yeats.

Among the early poems, the least defensive are those on historical or literary subjects.

It was a violent time. Wheels, racks, and fires
In every writer's mouth, and not mere rant.
Certain shrewd herdsmen, between twisted wires
Of penalty folding the realm, were thanked
For organizing spies and secret police
By richness in the flock, which they could fleece.

('A Mirror for Poets',
Fighting Terms, p. 28)

This is a different sort of poem, much richer in detail, much less preoccupied with abstract patterning. It is also a scholarly poem, packed with historical and literary references. The stanza on *King Lear* is especially notable:

Here in a cave the Paphlagonian King
Crouched, waiting for his greater counterpart
Who one remove from likelihood may seem,
But several nearer to the human heart.
In exile from dimension, change by storm,
Here his huge magnanimity was born.

Although it might be argued that the Paphlagonian King in Sidney's
Arcadia was not precisely 'waiting for' Shakespeare's Lear,[3] this is never-
theless not only a fine stanza but also good literary criticism. One of
Gunn's early strengths was the ability to mould a great deal of infor-
mation into his apparently effortless iambic pentameter: in 'A Mirror for
Poets' this ability is splendidly evident, even if a phrase like 'the diseased
and doubtful queen' (in the second stanza) seems to come a little too
easily. The final stanza describes a credo which underlies much of Gunn's
work, just as it underlies that of the Elizabethan poets:

In street, in tavern, happening would cry
'I am myself, but part of something greater.
Find poets what that is, do not pass by
For feel my fingers in your pia mater.
I am a cruelly insistent friend:
You cannot smile at me and make an end.'

The idea of 'happening' as 'a cruelly insistent friend' is one which
reappears in Gunn's later work.

The last poem from *Fighting Terms* which I want to examine here is the
sonnet 'Lerici', a poem which attempts to synthesise the packed, infor-
mative style of 'A Mirror for Poets' with elements of Gunn's more
abstract discursive mood. It does not entirely succeed.

Shelley was drowned near here. Arms at his side
He fell submissive through the waves, and he
Was but a minor conquest of the sea:
The darkness that he met was nurse not bride.

Others make gestures with arms open wide,
Compressing in the minute before death
What great expense of muscle and of breath
They would have made if they had never died.

Byron was worth the sea's pursuit. His touch
Was masterful to water, audience
To which he could react until an end.

Strong swimmers, fishermen, explorers: such
Dignify death by thriftless violence—
Squandering all their little left to spend.

(Fighting Terms, p. 27)

I have already referred to John Fuller's provocative and interesting
review of the third edition of *Fighting Terms:* Fuller comments in some

detail upon 'Lerici', and I find myself in close agreement with many of his remarks. He admires the opening, which 'seems to promise some striking central criticism of the poet'; but lines 5-8, he says, 'bring us back with a bump to the low tension of the explanatory style so common in the Fifties.' I think this is true, though it is more true of the language than of the content: compare the powerful directness of line 4 with the linguistic emptiness of line 8, where seven small words are doing nothing more interesting than acting as buttresses for 'made' and 'died'. The transition from 'Shelley' to 'Others' is an unhappy one, not because Gunn's unparticularised subjects are inherently less powerful than his specific ones (we have already seen that this is not the case), but because we are not told enough about the 'Others' once the transition has been made. Having fallen almost flat, the poem tries to revive itself by introducing the specific 'Byron': unfortunately, however, Byron turns out to be a mere cipher who might almost have come out of the catalogue of toughs in Gunn's later 'Lines for a Book'. In that later poem, a line like 'Dignify death with thriftless violence' might have seemed appropriate; here it seems awkward and unnecessary, the point too clumsily hammered home by the word 'thriftless' and the Elizabethan sexual pun in the final line. In spite of these reservations, beneath which the work of a lesser poet would probably sink without trace, Fuller is right to concede that 'Lerici' is a good poem, 'by no means the best he can do, but a sort of average'. It contains some of the best lines and some of the characteristic flaws of *Fighting Terms*.

2

If *Fighting Terms* is in many ways the most assured first collection of the fifties, a book which demonstrates not only a superficial grasp of the English tradition and its prosodic character but also a thorough commitment to the spirit of tough-mindedness which underlies it, Gunn's next two books *(The Sense of Movement* and *My Sad Captains)* can lay claim to equal though quite different distinctions. What impresses most about *The Sense of Movement* is the radicalism of subject-matter, a feeling that Gunn has firmly established his intellectual and technical abilities and is now able to go on to deal with the contemporary situation in a manner more confident than that of any other English poet writing at the time. Gunn has always been a shrewd judge of his own best work and, consequently, an able self-publicist: and just as his later volumes take their titles from outstanding poems so *The Sense of Movement* places itself explicitly in the centre of Movement poetry and at the same time indicates the intention, which Gunn has fulfilled with every book, of moving on.

To explain what I mean by the radicalism of *The Sense of Movement*, I want to start by considering one of the lesser poems in the book, 'Elvis Presley'. To find a poem about a rock musician in a book published by a traditional English poet in 1957 is odd enough, but Gunn's rigorous and serious approach to his subject is odder still. The approach is complex. Phrases like 'gangling finery', 'crawling sideburns', 'hackneyed songs', seem to indicate an expected degree of disdain on the poet's part; but 'Unreeling from a corner box' or 'We keep ourselves in touch with a mere dime' reveal a closer commitment, assuring us that Gunn is writing not from a detached or elevated position but from a personal involvement with the scene (this sort of ambivalence is characteristic of the book—the case of the motorcyclists in 'On the Move', where Gunn is at once with them and outside them, is exactly similar). And Gunn's complicated mixture of involvement and distancing is entirely appropriate to his subject.

'Elvis Presley', besides predicting the seriousness with which pop culture would later be treated and providing the title for George Melly's book on the subject *(Revolt into Style)*, embodies an unusual number of Gunn's preoccupations. The idea of limitation—'The limitations where he found success'—recurs in other poems, notably (or notoriously) 'The Beaters'. The notion of the divided or disembodied self—'Our idiosyncrasy and our likeness'—appears most clearly in poems such as 'The Corridor' and 'The Monster' from *My Sad Captains*. 'Impulse' and 'habit' are polarities which look very like human will and natural order in 'The Unsettled Motorcyclist's Vision of his Death'. And the concept of the pose, to which the last stanza is devoted, is already familiar, above all from 'Carnal Knowledge'. Indeed, this final stanza is at once an extension and a compression of the earlier poem:

> Whether he poses or is real, no cat
> Bothers to say: the pose held is a stance,
> Which generation of the very chance
> It wars on, may be posture for combat.

> *(The Sense of Movement,* 1957, p. 31)

The distancing is immaculate: the argument about the pose is subtly qualified by the phrase, 'no cat/Bothers to say'. Is the poet one such cat? We may suspect so, but he is not giving anything away here. The exact defining of the abstractions seems effortless: 'the pose held is a stance'—that is to say, the pose is momentary and willed but the stance permanent and habitual. But the stance, although now defined as inflexible, is itself 'generation of the very chance/It wars on', the prerequisite of the more transitory pose and therefore 'posture for combat'. The paradox is superbly managed, the resonances unmistakable though not over-insistent—'generation' has its sexual connotation, 'combat' its relationship with all the early poems in which love is seen in terms of warfare. And in building his well-structured metaphysical argument Gunn has thoroughly justified what may at first appear to be a perverse choice of subject.

Or has he? The web of cross-reference which can form around a poem like this one should warn us of one danger, Gunn's tendency to opt for a recurrent shorthand in both his imagery and his abstractions: some of the poems in *The Sense of Movement* seem to click into place with each other a little too mechanically, while the poet scuttles away under cover of his pose. Secondly, 'Elvis Presley', splendidly turned though it may be, begs a number of questions, some of which have been asked by John Fuller: 'Combat against what, we ask? What is the real significance of Presley? Or is the poet off on some erotic sidetrack, a piece of disguised butchery?' (Fuller, *loc. cit.*). It may be, and probably should be, argued that Fuller's questions are impertinent: that the poet has a right, which he exercises, not to answer them in his poem.

Nevertheless, a nagging doubt remains and is reinforced by 'Lines for a Book', placed adjacent to 'Elvis Presley' in *The Sense of Movement*. In his note on Gunn in *The Penguin Book of Contemporary Verse*, Kenneth Allott complains that some readers (he mentions Frank Kermode)[4] fail to see 'how unattractive such pieces as "Lines for a Book" or "The Beaters" really are' (*The Penguin Book of Contemporary Verse*, ed. Kenneth Allott, 2nd edition, 1962, p.374). Martin Dodsworth, discussing the poem and in a paradoxical way defending it, writes, 'It is *irredeemably* bad, not the sort of poem that can be patched up with a fresh adjective here, a new phrase there, and a revised conclusion' (Dodsworth, *op. cit.*, p.199). One gathers that Gunn has enjoyed the attacks which have been made on the poem: it has provided him with a notoriety which his Movement contemporaries conspicuously lacked.

Yet it seems to me that the subject-matter is not the most troublesome thing about 'Lines for a Book': its anti-intellectual brashness would no doubt have been applauded as irony had the poem been better made. As it stands, lines like,

I praise the overdogs from Alexander
To those who would not play with Stephen Spender.

or,

It's better
To go and see your friend than write a letter;
To be a soldier than to be a cripple;
To take an early weaning from the nipple
Than think your mother is the only girl. . . .

(*The Sense of Movement*, p. 30)

are as open to criticism for their crass rhymes and their thumping rhythm as they are for their content. After all, the poem is not entirely committed to thoughtless aggression: Gunn admits that the mind has 'got a place',

adding quite reasonably that
>It's not in marvelling at its mirrored face
>And evident sensibility.

Few readers would want to disagree with this assertion that the mind is
not self-sufficient but requires action to release its potential. One's more
legitimate quarrel is with the clumsiness of imagery and expression.

It is plainly absurd to consider 'Lines for a Book' as a complete (or even
completely sincere) statement of Gunn's intellectual creed, not least
because another and better poem in the book, 'To Yvor Winters, 1955',
modifies and clarifies such a statement. The fusion of thought and action,
hinted at among the banalities of 'Lines for a Book', is here expressed
much more convincingly:

>But sitting in the dusk—though shapes combine,
>Vague mass replacing edge and flickering line,
>You keep both Rule and Energy in view,
>Much power in each, most in the balanced two:
>Ferocity existing in the fence
>Built by an exercised intelligence.

>>(*The Sense of Movement*, pp. 44-45)

This is a lucid statement of faith in intellectual sanity as opposed to
romantic looseness and sentimentality: the ideal of 'an exercised intelli-
gence' is unexceptionable. The poem's conclusion is a vindication of
Winters' criticism and may also be seen as something of an apologia for
the excesses of 'Lines for a Book':

>Though night is always close, complete negation
>Ready to drop on wisdom and emotion,
>Night from the air or the carnivorous breath,
>Still it is right to know the force of death,
>And, as you do, persistent, tough in will,
>Raise from the excellent the better still.

Forceful attack is an essential part of the critic's equipment, not only to
weed out the feeble in existing literature but also to produce 'better still'
in the future: we could almost read this into 'Lines for a Book' too; almost,
but not quite, for 'Lines for a Book' fatally sacrifices Rule to Energy.

For Gunn at this time (as perhaps not in his later work) it is essential to
maintain this delicate balance between Rule and Energy: he treads his
chosen tightrope with spectacular flair, and he topples off spectacularly
too. In *The Sense of Movement*'s opening and most famous poem, 'On the
Move', he balances remarkably well. Partly, this is because he starts from
an unusually concrete situation:

>The blue jay scuffling in the bushes follows
>Some hidden purpose, and the gust of birds
>That spurts across the field, the wheeling swallows,

Have nested in the trees and undergrowth.
Seeking their instinct, or their poise, or both,
One moves with an uncertain violence
Under the dust thrown by a baffled sense
Or the dull thunder of approximate words.

(*The Sense of Movement*, p. 11)

'The blue jay', the *singular* bird, is of course representative of all blue jays, all birds, for the singular noun is generic here; but it is also a very real bird, made tangible by the vitality of the descriptive language: 'scuffling', 'gust', 'spurts', 'wheeling swallows' ('wheeling' looks forward to the motorcyclists too). The abstract argument springs from a specific situation: furthermore, the subject of the second sentence ('One') is both singular and universal in exactly the same way as the blue jay. 'One' is the motorcyclist, the 'half animal' human, the seeker unsure of what he is seeking: 'their instinct, *or* their poise, *or* both'; all that is certain is that he cannot attain it.

The second stanza localises again, the pronoun shifts from 'one' to 'they', 'the Boys'. Once more, the descriptive vitality creates an actual scene:

Small, black, as flies hanging in heat, the Boys,
Until the distance throws them forth, their hum
Bulges to thunder held by calf and thigh.
In goggles, donned impersonality,
In gleaming jackets trophied with the dust,
They strap in doubt—by hiding it, robust—
And almost hear a meaning in their noise.

Even though this poem is so well known, it is worth stressing the way in which Gunn manages some difficult transitions in it: the first stanza is hardly connected to the second at all, apart from that carefully placed word 'thunder', linking 'one' and 'the Boys'; the motorcyclists themselves change almost imperceptibly from figures in a landscape to counters in an argument with the phrase 'donned impersonality', accurate as literal description of the leather jacketed cyclists but also setting up an unmistakable resonance from earlier Gunn poems about poses and masks.

The expected, necessary synthesis of the opposing images in the first two stanzas—birds and boys, as it were—comes in the third:

They scare a flight of birds across the field:
Much that is natural, to the will must yield.

But the triumph of the will (the phrase, with its overtones of Leni Riefenstal's film and Nazi Germany, seems nevertheless the right one) is incomplete: the 'uncertain violence' of the first stanza remains uncertain, as phrases like 'imperfectly control', 'part solution', 'half animal', 'Reaching no absolute' confirm. And this is where the poem's poise is

shaken; for, having set up two images and related them to each other with
splendid assurance, Gunn dares to abandon them both for a stanza of
abstraction:

It is a part solution, after all.
One is not necessarily discord
On earth; or damned because, half animal,
One lacks direct instinct, because one wakes
Afloat on movement that divides and breaks.
One joins the movement in a valueless world,
Choosing it, till, both hurler and the hurled,
One moves as well, always toward, toward.

The weakness is in the first part of the stanza. The 'solution' (to what?) is
not precisely clear. The beginning of the second sentence ('One is not
necessarily discord/On earth') is clotted, the syntax clumsily telescoped
beneath the weight of abstraction, like the end of 'Tamer and Hawk'. But
the stanza is redeemed just in time: partly by the very fluent linguistic
movement of the last three lines; partly by the striking though simple idea
that in choosing to join the movement one is 'both hurler and the hurled'.

The poem's own motion is thus reasserted and carries it to its
conclusion: 'birds and saints complete their purposes', presumably
because they have 'direct instinct', unlike 'The self-defined, astride the
created will'. The stanza begins with the particularised 'they', but reverts
in the last three lines to the explicitly universal 'one':

At worst, one is in motion; and at best,
Reaching no absolute, in which to rest,
One is always nearer by not keeping still.

Few things in the poem testify to its quality more clearly than this superb
conclusion; the ground has been very carefully prepared for the epi-
grammatic, summarising final line which is reminiscent, in force and
decisiveness, of Empson's 'Aubade': 'The heart of standing is we cannot
fly' (William Empson, *Collected Poems*, 1955, p. 49). But behind both
Empson in 'Aubade' and Gunn here stands Yeats; and if 'On the Move'
is, as I suspect it is, what is commonly called a great poem (that is, one
which continues to astonish and impress after repeated careful readings),
then it is a great poem in a Yeatsian way, flawed like many of Yeats' finest
poems by a slight over-insistence on the author's personal pre-
occupations and mythology. Like Yeats' major poems too, this one carries
with it some thematic poor relations: 'The Unsettled Motorcyclist's
Vision of his Death' and 'Black Jackets'.

Frederick Grubb, in his refreshingly terse book *A Vision of Reality*,
writes, 'In "The Unsettled Motorcyclist's Vision of his Death" the
solemn pomposity of the argument sorts oddly with the wilful childish-
ness of the event, as if dashing old Walt Whitman, out for a joy-ride, was
moralizing into the youth's ear' (Frederick Grubb, *A Vision of Reality*,

1965, p. 206). The rebuke is partly earned. The discrepancy between argument and event is heightened by the construction of the poem which is, especially at the start, disconcertingly jingly:

> Across the open countryside,
> Into the walls of rain I ride.
> It beats my cheek, drenches my knees,
> But I am being what I please.

> (*The Sense of Movement*, p. 28)

This is not an auspicious start, and the hostile reader is unlikely to be placated by the statement about human will in lines 7-8, which is a less effective version of stanza four in 'On the Move', or by the existential shorthand of lines 11-12. Nevertheless, the poem improves as it becomes clear that the will versus nature conflict is to be worked out in descriptive rather than in abstract terms: even the word 'unsettled' in the title, which might at first have appeared to be abstract, comes to mean 'unseated' too. The reader is made to share the motorcyclist's feeling of discovery at the 'Gigantic order in the rim/Of each flat leaf'; and the aptness of 'accelerates', in which literal and metaphysical description are precisely combined, is impressive.

The latter part of the poem—which may more accurately be described as a 'vision' than the former—deals with nature's gradual assimilation of the motorcyclist. Now he is at the mid-point, 'Where death and life in one combine'; and by the end of the poem, the human will, which earlier could not 'submit/To nature though brought out of it', will have been entirely absorbed:

> Cell after cell the plants convert
> My special richness in the dirt.

For once in Gunn, the natural cycle is completed. Nature wins. But the last two lines of the poem, awkwardly separated by a stanza break for extra emphasis, suggest the limitation of that victory:

> All that they get, they get by chance.
> And multiply in ignorance.

One is reminded of Grubb's comment about 'solemn pomposity': the full-stops and the stanza break point just too glibly at the poem's 'message', and the result is strident and self-conscious.

Much the same could be said about the other bike-poem, 'Black Jackets'. The poem works well enough as a vivid, clear description until its last two stanzas; although it is hard not to feel that Gunn is paraphrasing himself too easily in lines like, 'Concocting selves for their impervious kit'. Again, it is Gunn's striving for an epigrammatic conclusion which leads him to brashness and to bathos:

> He recollected his initiation,
>   And one especially of the rites.
> For on his shoulders they had put tattoos:

> The group's name on the left, The Knights,
> And on the right the slogan Born to Lose.
>
> *(My Sad Captains*, 1961, p. 30)[5]

It is not difficult to see what has gone wrong here. Those two slogans, no matter how authentic or significant, seem altogether arbitrary, over-emphasised by the self-advertising final rhyme.

All these poems deal with, or at least imply, the limitations of the will: and this is the theme of 'Innocence', one of the most memorable poems in the first part of *My Sad Captains*. Gunn seems to see the subject more clearly when he has isolated it from his more usual imagery of motor-cyclists. The will here is personified by an unspecified 'He', and it is important that for the first four stanzas he should remain unparti-cularised. 'He' is plainly young; has 'The egotism of a healthy body'; is 'ignorant of the past'; 'what he possessed/Was rich, potential, like the bud's tipped rage'. The first two stanzas contain nothing which is incompatible with the ideals of the 'all-American boy' or the English public school. The next two stanzas narrow the field only slightly:

> The Corps developed, it was plain to see,
> Courage, endurance, loyalty and skill
> To a morale firm as morality,
> Hardening him to an instrument, until
>
> The finitude of virtues that were there
> Bodied within the swarthy uniform
> A compact innocence, child-like and clear,
> No doubt could penetrate, no act could harm.
>
> *(My Sad Captains*, p. 22)[6]

By now we can see that what at first might have appeared as virtues are in fact limitations; the subject is a member of a military organisation (we are perhaps intended to envisage something as apparently innocuous as a school CCF), but no further clue is given. Because the argument has been kept to an unspecified subject, the abstractions are unobtrusive and the paradoxes—'morale'/'mortality', 'swarthy uniform'/'compact innocence'—do not in any way strain the poem's quietly controlled diction (only 'it was plain to see' is pure padding). Although Gunn has firmly implied his reservations about this military training, the last two stanzas are in a real sense shocking:

> When he stood near the Russian partisan
> Being burned alive, he therefore could behold
> The ribs wear gently through the darkening skin
> And sicken only at the Northern cold,
>
> Could watch the fat burn with a violet flame
> And feel disgusted only at the smell,
> And judge that all pain finishes the same
> As melting quietly by his boots it fell.

There could hardly be more eloquent evidence to suggest that Gunn does not uncritically admire the cult of 'will'. And the construction of the poem makes it far more wide-reaching than any mere attack on Naziism. 'Implicit in the grey is total black,' writes Gunn in 'To Yvor Winters, 1955'; implicit in any militaristic system is this kind of 'innocence'. We are moved and astonished by the poem as by a stunning dramatic denouement: it succeeds exactly where 'The Unsettled Motorcyclist's Vision of his Death' and 'Black Jackets' fail, partly because the subject is more deserving of our concerned attention, partly because the verse is handled so carefully, the argument unfolded so deliberately.

Bearing in mind the distinguished success of 'Innocence', we may pause to wonder why so many of Gunn's poems at this time are flawed by brash clumsiness. The answer, I suggest, is that in the poems I have been considering here Gunn is trying to do something which is exceedingly though perhaps not obviously difficult. He is trying, much of the time, to find a contemporary equivalent of the Elizabethan 'plain style'. He is hindered by a number of factors: the lack of a readily identifiable diction (an especially acute problem for an English poet living in the United States); the intransigence of contemporary subject-matter; the lack, in modern Anglo-American vernacular, of that elegance which we may come across in even the plainest Elizabethan writing. In what I am rather arbitrarily delineating as Gunn's second phase (that is, *The Sense of Movement* and the first part of *My Sad Captains*), these problems are intrusive and at least partly unresolved: the sparser style which begins in the syllabic second part of *My Sad Captains* (though prefigured in 'Vox Humana') represents a different, arguably more successful approach to these same problems. The quest for a contemporary plain style is not, of course, confined to Gunn: J. V. Cunningham, a poet much admired by Yvor Winters, has sought it, leaning heavily on the Jonsonian paradigm; very different American poets, such as Robert Creeley and (particularly) Edward Dorn, have sought it in a terse and telescoped colloquialism; Donald Davie has sought and perhaps found it in a style which has become increasingly pared-down over the years but which at best still retains the unmistakable resonance of the speaking voice; and a number of younger English poets, who would recognise most or all of the writers I have just mentioned as influences on their work, have sought it.

The tracking down of influences, which can be a pointless business, has relevance when we are dealing with as consciously literary a poet as Gunn. As I suggested in my earlier remarks, Gunn seems to have willingly received stylistic transfusions from the Elizabethan poets on the one hand and from Yeats (and, by extension, Auden, Muir) on the other. The latter influences may get in the way of the 'plain style' but they also mitigate his abstract discursiveness, and the marriage of styles seems happiest in a poem such as 'Autumn Chapter in a Novel'. Gunn does not specify which novel, any more than he tells us which book his 'Lines' are for, but the situation owes much to *Le Rouge et le Noir*. The poem, quite unusually for Gunn, manages to *charm:* the tone (of the novel or type of novel as well as of the poem) is discreetly set in the first stanza:

Through woods, Mme Une Telle, a trifle ill
With idleness, but no less beautiful,
Walks with the young tutor, round their feet
Mob syllables slurred to a fine complaint,
Which in their time held off the natural heat.

(The Sense of Movement, p. 24)

The fusion of fallen leaves and words works exactly here, and will continue to work throughout the poem: the cleverness of the image does not disrupt the balance of the diction. A little later in the poem, the husband appears, talking about poachers to his bailiff: and again Gunn sets up his images (tutor/poacher, wife/'property') with impressive confidence. At the end of the poem, or the chapter,

They leave at last a chosen element,
Resume the motions of their discontent;
She takes her sewing up, and he again
Names to her son the deserts on the globe,
And leaves thrust violently upon the pane.

The argument of the poem is complete: earlier, we had been asked to 'suppose' that the leaves would settle again 'In much the same position as they rose', and indeed nothing has changed on the surface. Only the leaves thrusting 'violently upon the pane' hint at an increased tension which is exactly appropriate to this kind of novel.

'In Praise of Cities' attempts a similar parallel argument, only less successfully. Whereas Gunn was able to link words and leaves without obvious or ludicrous discrepancies, the linking of city and prostitute is more difficult. The poem swerves in two directions. First, it becomes over-abstract:

You welcome in her what remains of you;
And what is strange and what is incomplete
Compels a passion without understanding,
For all you cannot be.

(The Sense of Movement, p. 33)

These are perfectly acceptable lines, and they are quite effective in their context, but they tell us airily little we do not already know. Towards the conclusion, however, Gunn more or less abandons his parallel images, concentrating on the city itself though at the same time moving into a maze of allusions, and the poem gains in forcefulness as a result:

She wanders lewdly, whispering her given name,
Charing Cross Road, or Forty-Second Street:
The longest streets, desire that never ends,

> Familiar and inexplicable, wearing
> Cosmetic light a fool could penetrate.
> She presses you with her hard ornaments,
> Arcades, late movie shows, the piled lit windows
> Of surplus. Here she is loveliest;
> Extreme, material, and the work of man.

What began as a poem with metaphysical intentions has now become a purely descriptive one (although it could be argued that the metaphysicality is maintained to the end, it must be admitted that it has become extremely tenuous and distracting, and we are better off without it). 'In Praise of Cities' is one of the poems in which Gunn's early style is pushed to its limits and found to be less than completely satisfactory: hence, perhaps, the echoes of Wordsworth ('She wanders lewdly. . .' is surely a pastiche of 'I wandered lonely. . .'); possibly of Auden (though Auden sat 'in one of the dives/On Fifty-Second Street', not Fourty-Second Street); and of Eliot in 'Gerontion'. It is the sort of poem, one imagines, which precipitated the very deliberate changes of style in the second part of *My Sad Captains*.

The ambivalence and reflexiveness which are, as we have seen, characteristic of Gunn's work at this time are perhaps most fully evident in 'The Corridor'. A voyeur kneels at a keyhole in a dark hotel corridor; at the end of the corridor, a pierglass shows 'Dark, door, and man, hooped by a single band.' Already, as in 'Innocence', we feel the poem closing in around us, revealing itself cautiously and exactly.

> Pleasure was simple thus: he mastered it.
> If once he acted as participant
> He would be mastered, the inhabitant
> Of someone else's world, mere shred to fit.

> *(The Sense of Movement, p. 59)*

The pattern, like that of 'Tamer and Hawk', develops from an ambivalent exchange of roles. But now Gunn adds a third level: the voyeur notices in the glass 'Two strange eyes in a fascinated face/That watched him like a picture in a book.' The situation is complicated not merely by this third factor, but by a potentially infinite number of watchers:

> For if the watcher of the watcher shown
> There in the distant glass, should be watched too,
> Who can be master, free of others; who
> Can look around and say he is alone?

> Moreover, who can know that what he sees
> Is not distorted, that he is not seen
> Distorted by a pierglass, curved and lean?

Then, at the end of the poem:

> What could he do but leave the keyhole, rise,

Holding those eyes as equal in his eyes,
And go, one hand held out, to meet a friend?

We are not told whether the eyes in the glass are the voyeur's own eyes
(though we may suspect that they are): Gunn has selected his data with
extreme care and told us precisely what is necessary to clinch his
argument. We accept the poem on the poet's terms—and thus accept that
the argument itself is enough—or not at all. And if this provides evidence
of the poet's individuality, it also signals a danger: the poet is somehow
too insistent in 'The Corridor', so that we read the piece not as a poem but
specifically as a Gunn poem. 'The Corridor', too, with its emphasis on
distortion, reminds us—knowingly, no doubt—that the energy and
intelligence of these poems have brought with them distortions of sense,
of logic, of syntax from which relatively few ('On the Move', 'Innocence',
'Autumn Chapter in a Novel', perhaps) are free. The next phase of
Gunn's work represents a conscious effort to clarify and to pare down.
And if, as I have suggested, Gunn is aware that some fine poems of this
time are damaged by distortions, then I think it likely that 'The Corridor'
embodies as knowing and wry an irony as the title *The Sense of Movement*.
For the Elizabethans, a mirror; for Gunn, a pierglass.

3

It needs to be said rather firmly at this point that Gunn did not invent
syllabic metre, neither did he use it for the first time in the second part of
My Sad Captains. Nevertheless, this group of poems represents a
sustained and largely successful attempt to utilise a technique which
might have seemed to many readers the prerogative of the incompetent or
the slightly dotty. Modern English experiments with syllabics owe a great
deal to Robert Bridges' ideas about quantitative metre and to his
daughter, Elizabeth Daryush. Both Marianne Moore and W. H. Auden
have written a good deal in syllabics, though Miss Moore's syllabic counts
tend to be intuitive rather than mathematically accurate.

The first question to be asked is a disconcertingly bald one: why should a
writer who is capable of handling stress metres choose this apparently
perverse method of composition? Roy Fuller, in a lecture on syllabic
metre, gives the following answer:

The use of the technique, if not dictated by mere fashion, must reside
in providing an escape from iambic clichés, a chance of making a fresh
music. From the poet's point of view, as I can testify, the technique
can provide a way into the composition of a poem, particularly at the
dry start of a period of poetic productiveness, by freeing him from the
preliminary need to hear his subject, his *donnée*, his initial obser-
vation or image, as song—or at least the often elusive song of
traditional stress metre. No doubt this is due partly to the funda-

mentally simpler mathematics of syllabic metre, partly to the closeness
in tone and rhythm of the finished poem to its prosaic origins.

(Roy Fuller, *Owls and Artificers*, 1971, p.54)

This is agreeably sensible, though one must note that the argument holds
only for syllabics as an alternative to stress metre and takes no account of
free verse. We may, I think, suspect that Fuller's point about 'the dry
start of a period of poetic productiveness' is a relevant one in Gunn's case:
certainly Gunn's group of syllabic poems opens very deliberately with a
sense of discovery, a fresh start. The poems are prefaced by an epigraph
from Scott Fitzgerald.

I looked back as we crossed the crest of the foothills—with the air so
clear you could see the leaves on Sunset Mountains two miles away.
It's startling to you sometimes—just air, unobstructed uncompli-
cated air.

(F. Scott Fitzgerald, *The Last Tycoon*,
quoted in *My Sad Captains*, p. 35)

This epigraph seems to introduce not only the second half of *My Sad
Captains* but the whole body of Gunn's subsequent work, up to and
beyond his 1974 pamphlet collection *To the Air*. Gunn has also almost
certainly in mind Kenneth Koch's poem 'Fresh Air' (*The New American
Poetry*, ed. Donald M. Allen, 1960, pp. 229-236): parts of Koch's poem,
such as 'Blue air, fresh air, come in, I welcome you. . .' and 'farewell, stale
pale skunky pentameters. . .' are very close to Gunn's intentions here.
The strong sense of resolution is confirmed by the first poem, 'Waking in
a Newly-Built House. The title[7] seems to acknowledge that Gunn has not
himself built the syllabic house, carrying forward the feeling of discovery
from the Fitzgerald epigraph; and there is an unmistakable echo of Auden
too:

Harrow the house of the dead; look shining at
New styles of architecture, a change of heart.

(W. H. Auden, *Collected Shorter Poems
1930-1944*, 1950, p. 20. Not in subsequent editions)

The poem is a sort of manifesto for this 'change of heart':

It wakes me, and my eyes rest on it,
sharpening, and seeking merely all
of what can be seen, the substantial,
where the things themselves are adequate.

(*My Sad Captains*, p. 37)

'It' is a window, 'a wide pane in the bare/modern wall'. This vision
excludes equally the ornamental and the metaphysical, though not the
coyly paradoxical ('seeking merely all/of what can be seen'); Gunn
stresses the adequacy of 'things themselves', but one feels that these are
almost 'things' in a Wordsworthian sense, with a life of their own:

. . . that serene and blessed mood,

> In which the affections gently lead us on,
> Until, the breath of this corporeal frame,
> And even the motion of our human blood
> Almost suspended, we are laid asleep
> In body, and become a living soul:
> While with an eye made quiet by the power
> Of harmony, and the deep power of joy,
> We see into the life of things.   (Wordsworth, 'Tintern Abbey')

This tranquillity has much in common with the Fitzgerald epigraph and the Gunn poem, yet Gunn refuses to invest his things with Wordsworthian meanings, insisting at the end of the poem that their significance resides in their lack of significance, their arbitrariness:

> Calmly, perception rests on the things,
> and is aware of them only in
> their precise definition, their fine
> lack of even potential meanings.

'Waking in a Newly-Built House' works well enough as a manifesto setting out new ideals of sparseness and clear vision, and it seems to be just the sort of poem to which Fuller was referring in his Oxford lecture quoted above. But it must be admitted that this kind of writing can easily become tiresome, and that a 'lack of even potential meanings' is not on the face of things a very promising subject for poetry. Furthermore, syllabic poems tend to be remarkably unmemorable except where the syllabic pattern happens to coincide roughly with a stress metre (as in the first line of the last stanza quoted above). Perhaps for these reasons, there are few long poems in syllabics: it is worth noting that J. V. Cunningham's extended sequence *To What Strangers, What Welcome* effectively uses both syllabic and stress metre to sustain its vitality, and that Cunningham, like Gunn, has a clear notion of the function of syllabics:

> I write only to say this,
> In a syllabic dryness
> As inglorious as I feel. . .

> (J. V. Cunningham, *Collected
> Poems and Epigrams*, 1971, p. 105)

The thought of *Paradise Lost* or *The Prelude* rewritten in syllabics is not an obviously attractive one.

The case against Gunn's syllabic poems is quite neatly expressed in a poem by Alan Stephens, called 'The Vanishing Act' and subtitled 'syllabics for T. G.':

> After he concluded that
> he did not wish to raise his
> voice when he spoke of such mat-
> ters as the collapse of the
> Something Empire, or of things

the folk suffer from, he sim-
ply set in words such meanings
as were there, and then, when he

finished the final verse, van-
ished in the blank below it:
he'll reappear only on

the next page (not written yet).

(Alan Stephens, *The Sum*, 1958, p. 38)

One of the points which Stephens seems to be making here (and one
which perhaps has some validity) is that there is a discrepancy between so
prosaic a form as syllabic metre and so elevated a subject as 'the collapse
of the/Something Empire': the sparseness which suits 'Waking in a
Newly-Built House' so well is arguably less appropriate to a poem like
'My Sad Captains'. In theory, this line of argument has common-sense
on its side; in practice, it is precisely the distance between form and
subject which makes 'My Sad Captains' one of Gunn's most successful
poems.

The title is from *Antony and Cleopatra*. Antony, having sent Caesar's
messenger Thidias back to him and having regained his temper and his
optimism, is speaking to Cleopatra:

I will be treble-sinew'd, hearted, breath'd,
And fight maliciously: for when mine hours
Were nice and lucky, men did ransom lives
Of me for jests: but now, I'll set my teeth,
And send to darkness all that stop me. Come,
Let's have another gaudy night: call to me
All my sad captains, fill our bowls once more;
Let's mock the midnight bell.

(*Antony and Cleopatra*, III:13:178-185)

A good deal of this context is carried over into the poem; and the word
'sad' in the title may be taken to mean 'serious' or possibly even
'steadfast', as it does in *Antony and Cleopatra*.

One by one they appear in
the darkness: a few friends, and
a few with historical

names. How late they start to shine!
but before they fade they stand
perfectly embodied, all

the past lapping them like a
cloak of chaos. They were men
who, I thought, lived only to
renew the wasteful force they
spent with each hot convulsion.
They remind me, distant now.

> True, they are not at rest yet,
> but now that they are indeed
> apart, winnowed from failures,
> they withdraw to an orbit
> and turn with disinterested
> hard energy, like the stars.
>
> (*My Sad Captains*, p. 51)

One is immediately struck by the way in which the supposedly neutral syllabic form carries here an intense tone of reverie (to risk a possibly archaic word): the poem demonstrates forcefully that if syllabic metre can make a poem seem prosaic it can also, and for much the same reasons, add fluency and continuity. Coming as it does at the very end of *My Sad Captains*, the poem effectively conveys the idea of Gunn being revisited by his heroes: loyal they have certainly been, but they have changed nevertheless since 'Lines for a Book'. And Gunn has changed too, as he signifies by the carefully placed 'I thought' in the second stanza. What they remind him *of* (his past? his earlier brashness?) is not made clear: the train of thought peters out and is supplanted by the reflection that 'they are not at rest yet'. The conclusion is typically balanced and ambivalent: the captains are not defeated, for they have chosen to withdraw; just as, one assumes, Gunn has chosen to withdraw from them.

The other poem of this group which is most often mentioned in critical discussions of Gunn is 'Considering the Snail': rightly so, since it differs considerably from 'My Sad Captains' despite its superficial similarities. One is almost tempted to say that this poem really *is* prose. Gunn himself, in an interview published in 1964, was well aware of the risks involved in writing syllabic verse:

> There is a great danger in syllabics, that it will just fall into a mass of prose written differently, but I don't think good syllabics should do this any more than good free verse. I think one has got to be very open-minded about this and judge it by the end effect of each poem. In my own case, I find that in syllabics I can much more easily record the casual perception, whereas with metrical verse I very often become committed to a particular kind of rather taut emotion, a rather clenched kind of emotion.
>
> (Ian Hamilton, 'Four Conversations',
> *London Magazine*, New Series,
> IV:8, November 1964, p. 65)

In 'Considering the Snail', the proximity to prose is quite deliberate: there is a difference between

> The snail pushes through a green night, for the grass is heavy with water and meets over the bright path he makes, where rain has darkened the earth's dark,

and

The snail pushes through a green
night, for the grass is heavy
with water and meets over
the bright path he makes, where rain
has darkened the earth's dark.

(*My Sad Captains,* p. 39)

and it is the slightness of the difference which is interesting. On one level, the verse forces us to pause, ask questions, search out possible ambiguities. 'The snail pushes through a green'? A green what? Or just a green? On another level, the syllabic pattern cuts across the syntactical structure, making, in Roy Fuller's words, 'a fresh music'. What is certain is that the syllabic metre in 'Considering the Snail' gives to the poem a tentative, hesitating, questioning movement which mirrors the movement of the snail itself.

The remarkable alteration in tone which we find in the second part of *My Sad Captains* and in many of Gunn's subsequent poems is not, of course, purely a matter of syllabics though syllabic metre is the means Gunn adopts to delineate his 'change of heart'. Another, and less aridly prosodic, distinction which can be made is Martin Dodsworth's between the 'aggressive' technique of the earlier poems and the 'seductive' technique of the later ones. 'The transition,' says Dodsworth, 'is marked by the substitution of W. C. Williams and Marianne Moore for Yeats as poetic models' (Dodsworth, *op. cit.,* p. 204). I think this is drastically oversimplifying the matter of Gunn's influences, but the more general point that Gunn turned away from English models to American ones in his quest for a plain style is surely valid. John Fuller, writing in 1962 (an important point, for one suspects that he would not say quite the same things now), noticed the same tendency and remarked on it with disapproval:

Other landscapes and grotesqueries in the latest American manner fill the second part of *My Sad Captains.* The best of them ('Blackie, the Electric Rembrandt' and 'A Trucker') are, say, as good as good Corso, but one feels slightly discomfited, as though Gunn had dyed his hair.

(John Fuller, *loc. cit.*)

But surely a poetic dyeing of the hair (to retain Fuller's curious image) is what we have come to expect from major writers: it is what we find in Yeats's masks or, in a different way, Auden's revisions of his work. And it is, of course, temporary if the poet so chooses.

In the event, Gunn has not become in any constricting sense a syllabic poet; indeed, he now says he has entirely abandoned syllabics:

What I *have* given up is syllabics: I find the virtues of syllabics indistinguishable from those of free verse, so one might as well write free verse and trust entirely in the rhythms rather than partly in the number of syllables.

(Thom Gunn, reply to questionnaire
on rhythm, *Agenda*, X:4/XI:1,
Autumn-Winter 1972-3, p. 23)

Many of the pieces in his fourth collection, *Positives*, are more or less
syllabic, though without the earlier mathematical stringency: this is
without doubt the loosest collection of poems he has published, perhaps
necessarily and therapeutically so. Each poem in *Positives* faces a related
photograph by Ander Gunn: one might have suspected that Thom Gunn
would allow the photographs to do the descriptive work and tackle more
abstract matters in the poems; but this is not the case. Most of the poems
are descriptive, often rather flatly, and they are mostly brief and desultory
in manner. It sounds an unpromising book and the original hardback
edition had an unusually short life in its publisher's list. Few critics
bothered to take it seriously, but one of the few was Martin Dodsworth
(perhaps Gunn's most sympathetic commentator) in an essay in *The
Review:* 'In fact, *Positives* marks an important stage in Gunn's develop-
ment as a poet and has a special value for the reader in helping him to
understand the kind of poetry Gunn writes' *(The Review,* No.18, 1968,
p. 46). A little later on, Dodsworth remarks, 'On his own terms the poet's
experiment is a success, but the terms themselves provide him with only a
narrow space in which to work'—a comment which sounds, aptly
enough, like a paraphrase of a line from 'Elvis Presley': 'The limitations
where he found success'.

The value of *Positives* is that Gunn has learned to write flatly, undemon-
stratively, and loosely in a metrical sense; some of these poems fulfil the
promises of 'Waking in a Newly-Built House' more clearly than anything
in *My Sad Captains:*

> He rides up and down, and around:
> All things are means to wheely ends.
> All things radiate from the spokes under
> that hard structure of bars crossing
> precisely and usefully. But another
> leans against an iron fence, grown
> older, and dreams of cars.

(Positives, 1966, p. 16)

This is a complete poem, and it is not a particularly distinguished one. It
faces (as one could no doubt guess) a photograph of a bicycle shed
crammed with bicycles, and two young men—one astride a bicycle, the
other leaning against a fence. But one must be cautious about dismissing
the poem as pointless or redundant: I have just summarised the contents
of the photograph, rather baldly, but I have not in doing so summarised
the poem. The photograph states; the poet speculates, interprets in
appropriately gritty terms.

Other poems move interestingly away from their photographs; the subject of this one is sitting in a café:

> Youth is power. He knows it,
> a rough young animal, but
> an animal that can smile.
>
> He growls playfully, shaking
> dew from the bushes
> as he pokes his way through them
> into the world beyond,
> at ease in his power. For
> can there be limits?
>
> He makes, now,
> a fine gesture, inviting
> experience to try him.

(Positives, p. 20)

The subject-matter is close enough to Gunn's earlier territory for the contrast in tone to be striking, the brashness replaced by gentleness or what Dodsworth calls 'seductiveness'. And this tone enables Gunn to widen his range of subject-matter very considerably, as the final poem in the book shows:

> Something approaches, about
> which she has heard a good deal.
> Her deaf ears have caught it, like
> a silence in the wainscot
> by her head. Her flesh has felt
> a chill in her feet, a draught
> in her groin. She has watched it
> like moonlight on the frayed wood
> stealing toward her
> floorboard by floorboard. Will it hurt?
>
> Let it come, it is
> the terror of full repose,
> and so no terror.

(Positives, p. 78)

One can't imagine this sparse and moving poem fitting into any of Gunn's earlier collections: the extension of his poetic range to include old age and death (there are a number of pieces on these subjects in the book) would in itself go a long way towards justifying *Positives*. Formally, too, this poem is a logical development from *My Sad Captains:* the first eight lines are in the familiar syllabic sevens, but Gunn is now able to break away from the mathematical limitations of the form in the final lines; unrhymed, the poem is nevertheless held together firmly by half-assonances (about/caught/draught, for instance, or wood/to-ward/floorboard). Altogether it is a confident piece of writing, demonstrating Gunn's ability to move on from the Movement; and demonstrating by implication how sound the Movement was as a starting-point.

4

With *Positives,* Gunn's technical range—from tightly-structured, abstract metrical poems to descriptive free verse—is in one sense complete: his three subsequent volumes, his interesting retrospective pamphlet *The Missed Beat,* and his uncollected poems tend to consolidate rather than to expand this range. 'Touch', for instance, uses much the same kind of short-lined free verse as many of the pieces in *Positives,* but in a far more personal situation:

You are already
asleep. I lower
myself in next to
you, my skin slightly
numb with the restraint
 of habits, the patina of
self, the black frost
of outsideness, so that even
unclothed it is
a resilient chilly
hardness, a superficially
malleable, dead
rubbery texture.

(Touch, 1967, p. 26)

This is a long way from 'Even in bed I pose'. What has happened most notably to the verse, apart from the abandoning of the metrical norm and rhyme-scheme, is a loosening of the syntax: so that in the long second sentence, the movement which might previously have been dictated by metre is sustained by the continuing flow of phrase in which the strongest punctuation mark is the comma (there are no colons or semi-colons at all in the poem). This flexibility allows an unusually free movement of ideas and shifts of perception or consciousness within the poem:

What I, now loosened
sink into is an old
big place, it is
there already, for
you are already
there, and the cat
got there before you, yet
it is hard to locate.
What is more, the place is

not found but seeps
from our touch in
continuous creation, dark
enclosing cocoon round
ourselves alone, dark
wide realm where we
walk with everyone.

Not surprisingly, this poem figures largely in Martin Dodsworth's argument about Gunn's aggressive early poems and seductive later ones; Dodsworth notes that the 'continuity is hesitant, the continuity of exploration and discovery' and goes on to comment specifically on the poem's conclusion:

> Gunn takes advantage of this at the very end of the poem, where he allows new meanings to explode on us in a process of 'continuous creation'. The 'dark/enclosing cocoon' changes to a 'dark/*wide* realm', from the exclusiveness of 'ourselves alone' to the inclusiveness of walking 'with everyone'.

>> (Dodsworth, *The Survival of Poetry*, pp. 200-201)

Dodsworth provides a full and interesting commentary on 'Touch', though his word 'changes' in the above quotation does not properly imply (as surely the poem does) the sense of paradox, the two states existing simultaneously.

'Touch' belongs very obviously to the more recent Gunn, to a poetic world in which things are unstable, fluid, flexible. But the collection which takes its title from the poem ranges widely over Gunn's several territories. In terms of space, *Touch* is dominated by the long sequence 'Misanthropos', but I am not convinced either by this or by the later sequences 'The Geysers' and 'Jack Straw's Castle' that projects of this size are well suited to Gunn's particular gifts. 'Misanthropos', despite its length, borrows and distorts devices from the poet's more formal short lyrics. For example, the insistence on very tenuous half-rhymes in parts I and X looks pedantic in a long poem: rhymes like rhythm/him/from or movement/present/print seem arbitrary, to say the least. And the renaissance echo devices of part II (hear/here, know one/no one, discussed/disgust) make their points clumsily. But 'Misanthropos' is a considerable achievement, an unusually confident attempt at an extended sequence; at best, image and structure fuse completely:

> Hidden behind a rock, he watches, grown
> As stony as a lizard poised on stone.

>> (*Touch*, p. 46)

Not all the poems in *Touch* are as effective as this. Some of the old preoccupations reappear, staler now. 'Bravery' concludes:

> . . . you are
> my monstrous lover, whom

I gaze at
every time I shave.

(Touch, p.17)

It is another mirror-image poem, reminding us of 'The Corridor' in *The Sense of Movement* and suffering in the comparison. A few poems look as though they might have been written to go with photographs in *Positives*, 'Taylor Street' for instance; although the more tightly-organised 'Pierce Street' is better. It is an exploratory poem, moving quietly and delicately through an empty house and evoking exactly the right mood. In the house, Gunn meets 'the soldiers of the imagination' (sad captains?):

They vigilantly preserve as they prevent
And are the thing they guard, having some time stood
Where the painter reached to make them permanent.
The floorboards creak.
        The house smells of its wood.
Those who are transitory can move and speak.

(Touch, p. 54)

In 'Pierce Street', the abstractions complement and enrich the poem's more concrete content. But abstractions are as liable as concrete images to become clichés—perhaps more so, since the vocabulary is more restricted—and there are signs of this happening in 'Confessions of the Life Artist'. But the former emblems of choice and will—the motor-cyclists of 'On the Move' and 'Black Jackets'—have faded. The landscape becomes bleaker: streets are more often deserted now, houses empty, the conflicts of the early poems resolved only in desolation. If there is a unifying theme to *Touch*, it is the predicament of a man finding himself alone in a world which ought to be populated—the last man in 'Misanthropos', the visitor to the empty house in 'Pierce Street', the prisoner in 'In The Tank':

A man sat in the felon's tank, alone,
Fearful, ungrateful, in a cell for two.
And from his metal bunk, the lower one,
He studied where he was, as felons do.

(Touch, p. 52)

The poem provides a useful synthesis of Gunn's discursive 1950s style and his post-*My Sad Captains* clarity.

The cell was clean and cornered, and contained
A bowl, grey gritty soap, and paper towels,
A mattress lumpy but not over-stained,
Also a toilet, for the felon's bowels.

The attention, both detached and exact if faintly risible, to objects here is recognisably part of the poetic programme announced in 'Waking in a Newly-Built House'. However, by the end of the poem, we are back to the relentless, densely-packed logic of Gunn's first two books:

The jail contained a tank, the tank contained
A box, a mere suspension, at the centre,
Where there was nothing left to understand,
And where he must re-enter and re-enter.

As one approaches the present time in discussing the work of a living
writer it becomes difficult, and very probably foolish or impertinent as
well, to attempt any kind of overall assessment. So in talking about
Gunn's poetry since *Touch* I intend only to try and identify a few
directions in his work which I have not yet dealt with fully. One (and this
is a fairly negative point) is to do with brashness and overstatement. I said
earlier that Gunn is a shrewd judge of his own work and that in particular
he has tended to take the titles of especially interesting poems for his later
collections (we have seen that this is true of *My Sad Captains* and of
Touch, and I think it is true too of *Moly* and possibly *Jack Straw's Castle*).
At the same time, when his judgement lets him down it does so spec-
tacularly. There were obvious and ludicrous lapses of taste in the first
edition of *Fighting Terms*, which Gunn later modified: the textual
changes are usefully listed in the original printing of John Fuller's 1962
review of the book (*The Review*, No.1., April/May 1962, p. 34) but not in
the reprint in *The Modern Poet*. (There is an interesting and quite
convincing justification of the early version, however, in Robin Skelton's
review of the 1962 edition. Skelton rightly identifies the general tendency
in Gunn's work: 'the crude force of some early poems has given way to the
urbanity of the later.' He argues that the 'exciting admission of common-
place locutions and vernacular stridencies into poetry that was at once
extroverted in tone and metaphysical in content . . . made Gunn's earlier
work invigorating and forward-looking'. *Critical Quarterly*, IV:3,
Autumn 1962, p.274.) I shall return shortly to Gunn's habit of revision,
when dealing with a much more recent poem, 'Fever'.

Disconcertingly ill-judged poems continue to appear long after *Fighting
Terms*, poems which are quite without subtlety (by which I do not
necessarily mean delicacy) or point. 'Lines for a Book' is the obvious
example; 'Black Jackets' is another, less strident one; and others have
rather understandably not appeared in book form. For instance, 'A Crab':

A crab labours across my thigh.
Oh. The first time I got crabs, I
experienced positively
Swiftian self-revulsion: me
unclean! But now I think instead
'I must get some A200,'
and feel (picking it up, watching
its tiny beige legs, a live thing
that wriggles in all directions)

neither disgust nor indifference,
but a fondness, as for a pet.
I'm glad it's nothing worse, and yet
it slipped and swung from one of us
to the other, unfelt because
the skin was alive with so much
else. It was a part of our touch.

(*London Magazine,* New Series,
I:11, February 1962, pp. 6-7)

Or 'Tending Bar':

With the impartial firm grace
   of good humour, you mix, pour,
   serve drinks through the muddled air,
wipe the bar, empty ashtrays,

and glance round your dependents.
   I wonder, does being shut
   behind the bar constitute
strength, or just its appearance?

But that's begging the question,
   as though I asked which you were
   —drinker or just bartender?
They are not exclusive. When

Cowboy Hat knocks back his stool,
   about to slug his small queer
   neighbour, you straightway appear
among the drinkers and, cool

as Jesus, tell him to leave.
   He hesitates, twice your size.
   Civil, contained, your style is
a power you need not prove

with smashed seating. You assert
   what might be, and then—since there
   is menace in lack of fear—
what is: he leaves, looking hurt.

(*Critical Quarterly,* VI:1, Spring 1964, pp. 33-34)

There are two things missing in these poems: music and humour. The
first deficiency is the less troublesome, since Gunn has shown himself
well able to repair it—though one might note that the two poems offer
impressive evidence for opponents of syllabics, for the metre forces some
really uncomfortable lines in each one. But the lack of humour is another
matter. G. S. Fraser wrote of Gunn, before the publication of 'A Crab' or
'Tending Bar', 'He is often a witty poet, in the sense of being concise and
epigrammatic, but he is never heartily familiar in tone' *(Critical*

Quarterly, III:4, Winter 1961, p. 359). And, later in the same essay, 'Gunn, as I have said, has plenty of wit of the severer kind, but almost no humour' (*ibid.*, p. 363). One does not expect from Gunn the apparently lightweight though usually double-edged jocularity of Larkin: but often it seems as if he doesn't know a trivial or humorous subject when he sees one (and consequently doesn't recognise the hilariously bathetic elements in a poem like 'In The Tank', discussed above).

Both poems deal with private situations; 'Tending Bar' is dedicated to Don Doody, so Gunn has a specific informed reader in mind there. Neither poem seems really concerned with communicating the situation, though there is an air of somewhat adolescent bravado about both of them: in each case, Gunn's intention seems to be to provide a pretext for a concluding statement (one has a strong sense of the conclusions coming first to the poet's mind and the supporting poems being added as a sort of scaffolding). In 'Tending Bar', the conclusion is neat enough in a characteristic way; in 'A Crab', Gunn is playing with an idea which is more fully realised in 'Touch'. In each case, the humourless, oddly embarrassed brashness ('I must get some A200', 'cool/as Jesus') is ruinous.

Unfortunately, there is evidence in Gunn's more recent work that he has not learned from these mistakes. The prize exhibit in *Moly* (one so evidently offered for attack by the poet that it is impossible to resist it) is a poem called 'Listening to Jefferson Airplane in the Polo Grounds, Golden Gate Park', which is a fairly lengthy title. I quote the poem in full:

> The music comes and goes on the wind,
> Comes and goes on the brain.

(Moly, 1971, p. 41)[8]

A natural reaction would be disbelief. One reviewer asked: 'Is this the famous blowing of the mind?' (Neil Rennie, *London Magazine*, New Series, XI:2, June/July 1971, p. 130). And that is probably the safest reaction, for one feels one is stepping directly into the poet's trap if one dares to wonder how the man who wrote probably the first and arguably the best poem on rock music ('Elvis Presley') could produce this.

But there is more, and conceivably worse, in *Moly*. 'Tom-Dobbin' is a sequence of four 'centaur poems', of which this is the second:

> Hot in his mind, Tom watches Dobbin fuck,
> Watches, and smiles with pleasure, oh what luck.
> He sees beyond, and knows he sees, red cows,
> Harsh green of grass, and pink-fired chestnut boughs.
> The great brown body rears above the mare,
> Plunging beneath Tom's interested stare.
>
> In coming Tom and Dobbin join to one—
> Only a moment, just as it is done:
> A shock of whiteness, shooting like a star,
> In which all colours of the spectrum are.

(Moly, p. 29)

The ludicrous banality of the verse—and of lines 2, 6, 8 and 10 in parti-
cular—cannot be other than intentional; one's difficulty lies in deciding
why Gunn intended it. And no very clear solution offers itself, except that
the poet seems to revel in his notoriety; this is as bad a poem as 'Lines for a
Book' and a far more self-conscious one.

   To be fair to Gunn, some of his worst poems (and some of his best)
remain uncollected and others have been extensively revised (though not
always with encouraging results). This habit of revision, which makes the
various editions of *Fighting Terms* so engrossing, has been at work again
on the poems in *To The Air* which are more or less contained in the first
section of *Jack Straw's Castle*. Rewriting may be a virtue or a necessity in
a style as plain as Gunn's: it is a part solution, after all. Plainness demands
accuracy but can lead to awkwardness, and Gunn's revisions attempt to
refine the one and dispel the other. Sometimes they are, rather char-
mingly, matters of fact: in 'The Corporal' he remembers being 'fourteen
or so' in *To The Air* but (ripeness is all) 'fifteen or so' in *Jack Straw's
Castle*. Elsewhere there are drastic cuts: 'The Geysers' (epigraph from
'To Penshurst', a poem of considerable importance for Gunn) loses a
whole long section, 'Discourse from the Deck', and this is probably just as
well for much of the poem is stilted, although there are patches of that
simple but instantly recognisable Gunnian pentameter:

   The gold hills, and a certain wooden deck
   Outside a bath house falling into wreck,
   Part shaded by wide figtrees, part in sun.
   Fig-musk pervades the thought of everyone.
                                        (*To the Air*, 1974, p. 17)

The most serious of these revisions, however, and the one which perhaps
causes a real casualty, concerns the poem called 'Fever'. The changes are
worth examining closely, for they interestingly reveal Gunn's problems
with a poem which, like 'Carnal Knowledge', has I think been damaged by
the author's wish to tidy it up. The version in *To the Air* consists of 28
lines, divided into two sections of eight and twenty lines respectively; the
version in *Jack Straw's Castle* is cut to 25 lines and divided into six, ten,
and nine lines. Apart from the removal of a stray syllable ('though') in line
three, the first five lines are similar in each version; lines four to six (i.e.
the second half of the first stanza) in *Jack Straw's Castle* are as follows:

   You change direction and shift from foot to foot,
      Too skittish to be capable of repose
         Or of deciding what is worth pursuit.
                                  (*Jack Straw's Castle*, 1976, p. 17)

In the previous version, the sentence ends after 'repose' and is followed
by the much stronger 'Like an allegorical figure of pursuit. . . .', but this
was bought at the cost of the remaining two lines of the stanza in *To the
Air*, now jettisoned, the first of which is especially awkward: 'Which can't

reach the end towards which it points its nose/And remain itself, you're unable to engage.' These deserved to go, but the 'pursuit' line has suffered badly as a result.

Worse misfortunes have befallen the rest of the poem, which was in the earlier version a single unit. Lengthy quotation is unavoidable here. First, the second stanza in *Jack Straw's Castle* (lines 7-16):

Your mother thought you beautiful, I suppose,
    She dandled you all day and watched your sleep.
Perhaps that's half the trouble. And it grows:
    An unattended conqueror now, you keep
Getting less beautiful toward the evening's end.
    The boy's potential sours to malice, deep
Most against those who've done nothing to offend.
    They did not notice you, and only I
Have watched you much—though not as covert friend
    But picturing roles reversed, with you the spy.

Knowing the early version, it's hard to be fair to this one: but surely it seems crudely stitched together, which is unsurprising in view of the surgery it has undergone, and curiously perfunctory. In fact, the most striking phrases and images have been ironed out in revision. The last two lines quoted above are retained intact from *To the Air;* otherwise, the earlier version of the corresponding lines is as follows:

Your mother thought you beautiful I suppose:
    Perhaps that's half your trouble at this age.
Oh how she dandled her pet and watched his sleep.
    Here no one watches the revolving stage
Where, joints and amyl in your pocket, you keep
    Getting less beautiful toward the evening's end.
Potential of love sours into malice now, deep
    Most against those who've done nothing to offend
Except not notice you, for only I . . .

                                        (*To the Air*, p. 9)

This is harsher, but it is the harshness which propels the poem. Almost all the changes are dilutions: the jibe about 'half *your* trouble' goes; 'Oh how she dandled her pet' loses its edge; 'the revolving stage' and 'joints and amyl', image and information, are out; 'Potential of love' becomes much more vaguely 'The boy's potential'; the essential logical connections, '*Except* not notice you, *for* only I', are filtered out. The versification suffers too: the removal of the age/stage rhyme forces in an extra rhyme for repose/suppose, the entirely superfluous 'And it grows'. The poem's remaining lines have survived with less mutilation, though the continuity of the *To the Air* version is interrupted by the stanza break followed by a pointless rhetorical question in *Jack Straw's Castle*. One other rewritten line towards the end seems a real improvement. Despite this, 'Fever' remains a moderately effective poem, if a clumsy one, weakened fatally by Audenesque rewriting.

A more interesting development in Gunn's recent writing is the one prefigured by 'Pierce Street' and to some extent by *Positives:* descriptive poetry of great delicacy, an extraordinary contrast with poems such as 'Tom-Dobbin'. 'The Fair in the Woods' is one such poem: Gunn the self-publicist tells us that it was written after using LSD (which is plain enough from the poem itself) but as a psychological or literary fact this does not seem especially relevant. (Many of the poems in *Moly* are concerned with drugs, specifically acid but also the mythological herb which gives the book its title; one may as well note, however, that Gunn had used drugs much earlier and that at least one and probably more of the poems in *My Sad Captains* were composed after taking mescalin.) 'The Fair in the Woods', with its visual subtlety, reads like one of Gunn's earlier poems about paintings ('Before the Carnival', 'In Santa Maria del Popolo'):

> The woodsmen blow their horns, and close the day,
> Grouped by some logs. The buckskins they are in
> Merge with ground's russet and with tree-trunk's grey,
> And through the colour of the body's skin
> Shift borrowings out of nearby birch and clay.

(Moly, p. 39)

The neutral tones—of colour, not of voice—are exactly indicated: the one oddity of colour, the grey tree-trunks, is resolved by the information in the last line that the trees are birches. The best parts of the poem are about colours merging, separating; the middle stanzas seem over-explicit, but the conclusion reaffirms the themes and the poetic strengths of the opening:

> Knuckle takes back its colour, nail its line.
> Slowly the tawny jerkins separate
> From bark and earth, but they will recombine
> In the autumnal dusk, for it is late.
> The horns call. There is little left to shine.

This is wonderfully poised and restrained, yet magically evocative. Even more impressive is 'Sunlight', the characteristically well-placed last poem in *Moly:*

> Some things, by their affinity light's token,
> Are more than shown: steel glitters from a track;
> Small glinting scoops, after a wave has broken,
> Dimple the water in its draining back;
>
> Water, glass, metal, match light in their raptures,
> Flashing their many answers to the one.
> What captures light belongs to what it captures:
> The whole side of a world facing the sun,

> Re-turned to woo the original perfection,
> Giving itself to what created it,
> And wearing green in sign of its subjection.
> It is as if the sun were infinite.
>
> (*Moly*, p. 53)

Although the plain style does not often make for strongly characterised verse, the poem of which this is the opening could not, I think, be mistaken for the work of any other writer. The supple transition from 'things' (again) to specific yet elemental examples of substances which seem to generate their own light and are thus 'more than shown', 'Flashing their many answers to the one' (a simple and stunningly effective line); the unforced movement back and forth between image and argument; the use of paradox ('What captures light belongs to what it captures') and pun ('Re-turned'): these are all characteristic strengths of Gunn's but they have seldom been used to such excellent effect. With the fourth stanza, the argument and the tone modulate:

> But angry flaws are swallowed by the distance;
> It varies, moves, its concentrated fires
> Are slowly dying—the image of persistence
> Is an image, only, of our own desires:
>
> Desires and knowledge touch without relating.
> The system of which sun and we are part
> Is both imperfect and deteriorating.
> And yet the sun outlasts us at the heart.

Not only do water, glass and metal only *seem* to produce their own light; the real source of light only *seems* to be perfect. Gunn in this way adds a new dimension to the argument, just as he did in 'The Corridor'. 'And yet the sun outlasts us at the heart', so Gunn can conclude the poem with an invocation:

> Great seedbed, yellow centre of the flower,
> Flower on its own, without a root or stem,
> Giving all colour and all shape their power,
> Still recreating in defining them,
>
> Enable us, altering like you, to enter
> Your passionless love, impartial but intense,
> And kindle in acceptance round your centre,
> Petals of light lost in your innocence.

This conclusion invites or risks comparison with Yeats' 'Among School Children' and, even if one does not share Yvor Winters' somewhat extreme view of the Yeats poem (see Chapter One), 'Sunlight' has nothing to fear from the comparison.

Both 'The Fair in the Woods' and 'Sunlight' embody a tone of wonder which becomes explicit in the title poem, dated 1967, of *The Missed Beat*,

a pamphlet of otherwise uncollected pieces spanning the years 1951 to
1967:

Above the harsh clods blanked-white in the sun
Where hour by hour
Ants labour one by one:
A petal-face of pinkish-red so sheer
That flux itself misses a beat.
I hold my breath. Bent here,
Absorbed in wonder, shaken by my power,
I try to stop the moment, this, complete:
Down of the flower
Seemed like the down that might invest
Both look and looked-at, being inseparable.
Can it be repossessed?
I feel my pulse's climb, and the long fall.

(The Missed Beat, 1976, unnumbered pages)

The poem seems only half-formed, which is not in this case necessarily a
disadvantage: what is caught is an unusually intimate meditation which
might well have been polished into a poem like 'Sunlight' but which is
here left for once in something like a raw state.

Most of the qualities of these poems, and at least one more, are also to be
found in an uncollected poem, 'North Kent':

Behind the Works, the chalk pits blurred with pocks
Trough hills where, higher, chalk still lies unbudged,
Bright porous clutch an inch below the thyme.
And in the foreground cylinders and blocks
Are of a whiteness in the same way smudged,
Or realised, by shadow, grease, and grime.

(The Listener, 22 February 1968)

The additional quality here is the extreme accuracy of local description;
but the parenthetical 'Or realised' ought to prepare us for the kind of
argument which will have developed by the last stanza:

The workmen carting sacks of dust through dust
Are clotted with the impurities they cause,
And are, bulk shaped against the pallor here.
Above, from chimneys that the fine grains crust,
Puffs of blanched smoke break, thinning where wind draws,
Escaping, pure and useless, as they appear.

Again, the parenthesis—'And are'—turns accurate description into
something more general and discursive. The poem is by no means
perfect: the rhymes have forced some clotted diction (an old and
recurrent fault of Gunn's); the ambiguous parentheses may be mere
vagueness. But it is recognisably the work of a very capable writer, as
some of the poems which have been included in Gunn's recent collections
are not.

Jack Straw's Castle, apart from the poems I have already mentioned, is bewilderingly various, and the variety is once again evidence of Gunn's poetic youthfulness. There is no single poem as instantly impressive in its absolute rightness and completeness as 'Sunlight' nor anything as completely daft as 'Listening to Jefferson Airplane'. Instead, a relaxed, even jokey tone predominates (though the humour is as heavy-handed as one would suspect from Gunn's earlier work): Gunn inhabits a range of improbable personae, from his dog in the very remarkable poem 'Yoko' to the self-explanatory 'An Amorous Debate: Leather Kid and Fleshly' which, like several other poems in the book, seems to owe something to Edward Dorn. The title sequence contains some impressive writing (particularly in the third section, which is also the most formal), though individual poems seem stronger than the structure into which they are organised and some connected links (like the seventh part of the 'Jack Straw' sequence) are perilously weak. The poems which benefit most from the sense of informality are the modest, evocative fragments of autobiography: 'Last Days at Teddington', 'Autobiography', 'Hampstead: The Horse Chestnut Trees'.

'Thom Gunn,' wrote Kenneth Allott, 'has some of the most valuable poetic gifts (intelligence in close alliance with sensibility, structural sense, a feeling for economy of phrase), but his future development appears to be quite exceptionally open' *(The Penguin Book of Contemporary Verse,* 2nd edition, p. 374). That note was written after the appearance of *The Sense of Movement,* before *My Sad Captains.* Much the same could be said now. Allott did not mean his comment to be an optimistic one, but it seems to me that Gunn's range and his ability to disconcert his readers have turned out to be assets, except in the case of a few disastrously ill-judged poems. These failures, like those of Donald Davie and Philip Larkin, may be attributable to a loss of confidence in his audience. Gunn has not ranged as esoterically in style or subject-matter as Davie nor remained as doggedly traditional as Larkin: but he has demonstrated more effectively than either of these writers the continuing vitality of a poetry which takes as its starting-point the English tradition as it was conceived by his former postgraduate tutor, Yvor Winters. And he has remained loyal to that tradition even as he has modified it: thus, when he lists among the characteristics of Jonson's 'To Penshurst', 'the coolness, the formality, the eschewing of any striking rhetorical techniques, the general sense of external occasion dominating the poem' (Introduction to *Poet to Poet: Ben Jonson,* 1974, p. 12), one is bound to notice how often these qualities are found in Gunn's own work. His is already an important poetic achievement: and if from time to time we are disconcerted by his weaker poems, we should perhaps bear in mind how indulgently we pass over the bad poems in a collected Wordsworth or Yeats.

NOTES

1. 'Auden must be, as far as direct imitation of style goes, the most influential poet of the century—and for obvious reasons: his casual and topical manner, in which any subject can be discussed with equal assurance, is obviously attractive to anyone learning how to write.' Thom Gunn, 'Three Poets', *Listen*, III:1, Winter 1958, p. 13.

2. Cf. Wyatt:

> I have sene theim gentill tame and meke
>> That nowe are wyld and do not remembre
>> That sometyme they put theimself in daunger
> To take bred at my hand; and nowe they raunge
> Basely seeking with a continuell chaunge.
>
> ('They fle from me . . .')

3. For the relationship between the story of the Paphlagonian king in the 'old' *Arcadia* (II:10) and Shakespeare's *King Lear*, see Kenneth Muir, Introduction to *King Lear*, 'The Arden Shakespeare' 1952, pp. xxxvii-xlii.

4. See Frank Kermode, review of *The Sense of Movement*, in *Listen*, II:4, Spring 1958, pp. 17-19.

5. *My Sad Captains* received some curious reviews: A. E. Dyson, for instance, described this ill-judged poem as 'very moving' and thought it, with 'In Santa Maria del Popula' *(sic)* 'equal [to] anything he has given us before.' *Critical Quarterly*, III:4, Winter 1961, p. 379.

6. The level tone and forceful content of this poem may be interestingly compared with Anthony Hecht, ' "More Light! More Light!" ', *The Hard Hours*, 1967, p. 64. For a very different estimation of 'Innocence', see Edward Lucie-Smith, 'The Tortured Yearned as Well', *Critical Quarterly*, IV:1, Spring 1962, pp.34-43. Lucie-Smith says, 'It would take a lot to persuade me that either "Innocence" or "The Beaters" are successful works of art.' His assumption that these two poems may be bracketed together seems to me mistaken, as my comments on 'Innocence' will indicate.

7. It may be significant that Gunn discarded the earlier and more localised title of the poem: 'Waking in a Newly Built House, Oakland', *Listen*, II:4, Spring 1958, pp. 2-3.

8. For an interesting (and largely convincing) defence of *Moly*, see Donald Davie, 'The Rhetoric of Emotion', *Times Literary Supplement*, 29 September 1972.

Chapter Three

DONALD DAVIE: POET AS CARPENTER

1

The point to be made firstly and cautiously about Donald Davie's poetic development is that it is in striking ways parallel to Gunn's. Caution is called for because no two creative writers worth reading can be described as parallel except in a superficial sense, and it is not my intention to substitute wild generalisation for attention to individual poems. Nevertheless, both poets were first published in book form by the Fantasy Press in 1954 and 1955; both appeared in *New Lines;* both developed away from the styles of the Movement in the early sixties; both have made California their home and taught at universities there; and both have clearly assimilated American influences into their work.

Davie is at once the most consistent and the most restless of contemporary English poets. His consistent concerns have been intellectual truthfulness and dedication to the craft of language. His restlessness has been both geographical and literary, and it has also been evident in his comments upon his own work and that of his contemporaries. In this sense, he has never been part of the Movement or of any other movement. Here, for instance, are three extracts from remarks made by him at various times on the poetry of the Movement; the first was written in reply to the comments in *Delta* on 'The New Movement' in 1956:

> Mr Amis, I'm afraid, and Mr Larkin would agree with you that 'the growing tendency for poets to write *about* painting or *about* poetry, a concern with art and imagery drawn largely from the arts, rather than with life, will only paralyse art.' I think you are, all three of you, wrong; and it's a pity when one finds a university magazine joining in the cry with *Encounter,* and promoting a vulgar error. Isn't the reading of a poem, or the seeing of a picture, an experience like any other? Isn't such an experience, for many people, unusually intense and meaningful? And what is this 'life' which you oppose to 'art'? If art is so disreputably [*sic*] and marginal an affair that poetry can afford to ignore it, why do we care about the art of poetry?
>
> (Delta, No.9, 1956, p. 28)

The second comes from an article called 'Remembering the Movement', published in 1959:

> We ridiculed and deprecated 'The Movement' even as we kept it going. I don't know, but I should imagine that this would have been the most baffling thing about us, to any Frenchman (say) or American, who got into company with two or three of us. For in their countries, so far as I can see, writers who set out in concert to write a chapter of literary history don't have to pretend elaborately to be doing something else. Why should they? We in the Movement did so, for the same reasons which brought the whole thing to a halt and broke it up before it was under way—out of pusillanimity: from the unforgivable literary sin of going much further than halfway to meet our readers, forestalling their objections, trying to keep in their good books. Ours was writing which apologized insistently for its own existence, which squirmed in agonies of embarrassment at being there at all. In the interstices of our poems—in the metrical places wasted on inert gestures of social adaptiveness—'no doubt', 'I suppose', 'of course', 'almost', 'perhaps'—you can see the same craven defensiveness which led us, when we were challenged or flattered or simply interviewed, to pretend that the Movement didn't exist, that it was an invention of journalists, that we had never noticed how Larkin and Gunn and Amis had something in common, or that, if we had noticed, it didn't interest or excite us.
>
> (Prospect, Summer 1959, p. 13)

And the third is from the 1966 'Postscript' to *Purity of Diction in English Verse:*

> I like to think that if the group of us had ever cohered enough to subscribe to a common manifesto, it might have been *Purity of Diction in English Verse.*
>
> It is a great pity, I think, that we did not acknowledge our common ground in some such way. Instead, we were all morbidly anxious not to seem to be acting in concert. This anxiety, I'm afraid, came from a streak of aggressive philistinism that ran through all our thinking. We would not entertain for a moment the idea that poetry could be, in some degree or from some points of view, a self-justifying activity. The merest whiff of art for art's sake, and we panicked, shouting.
>
> *Purity of Diction in English Verse,*
2nd edition, 1967, pp. 197-8)[1]

It is plain that in retrospect the Movement seems a much more unified affair to Davie than it did at the time (one notices that his later public disagreements with Larkin have their antecedents as far back as 1956). Davie seems always to have been troubled by that 'streak of aggressive philistinism' in the Movement. Consequently, his comment about 'the unforgivable literary sin of going much further than halfway to meet our readers' is a misleading one: some of his contemporaries may have done this, but not Davie himself—as he tacitly admits when he apologises for the obscurity of some of his early work in the 'Foreword' to his *Collected Poems 1950-1970* (1972, p. xv). Similarly, the claim that 'we panicked' at 'the merest whiff of art for art's sake' is hardly applicable to Davie himself: in my first chapter I noted Bernard Bergonzi's comment on the number of literary references in *Brides of Reason;* and Davie's 1956 reply to *Delta* is obviously an attempt to justify that sort of reflexive poem about art which he, but not Amis or Larkin, was writing at the time. (One need look no further than Amis's 'Something Nasty in the Bookshop' or Larkin's 'A Study of Reading Habits' for evidence of this contrast.)

Davie's allusive early poems no longer need elaborate apology (some of his more recent work is far more tightly packed with arcane references): the false note in *Brides of Reason* now seems to be the coyness which persuades the poet to describe himself as 'A pasticheur of late-Augustan styles, (*Collected Poems,* p. 1) and which flickers beneath the rightly well-known 'Remembering the Thirties'. This poem seems to have rebounded in interesting ways:

> They played the fool, not to appear as fools
> In time's long glass. A deprecating air
> Disarmed, they thought, the jeers of later schools;
> Yet irony itself is doctrinaire,
>
> And curiously, nothing now betrays
> Their type to time's derision like this coy
> Insistence on the quizzical, their craze
> For showing Hector was a mother's boy.
>
> A neutral tone is nowadays preferred.
> And yet it may be better, if we must,
> To praise a stance impressive and absurd
> Than not to see the hero for the dust.

(*Collected Poems,* p. 21)[2]

Davie's description of the thirties seems now—such is the effect of 'time's long glass'—to fit the fifties. The first stanza quoted above could be seen as providing an excuse for Larkin's line 'Books are a load of crap' (*The Whitsun Weddings,* 1964, p.31), an excuse which Davie, when writing specifically about Larkin, in fact refuses to accept (see *Thomas Hardy and British Poetry,* 1973, p. 79). And as for the 'neutral tone' which 'is nowadays preferred', this may arguably apply to Amis and to Larkin, but Davie himself certainly did not prefer it nor is it to be found in Gunn's work of the fifties which I discussed in Chapter Two.

The poems in *Brides of Reason* tend to be ironic, quizzical, allusive: there is little of the stridency of Gunn's first volume, *Fighting Terms,* in Davie's. Partly, no doubt, this is because Davie was older and had presumably written the poems over a longer period of time; and partly there is the feeling, which has often recurred in his work, of defensive-ness, of a man who has worked hard for his learning and who is not going to give it away easily. On the comparatively rare occasions in *Brides of Reason* when highly intelligent (and guarded) scholarship gives way to something more straightforwardly autobiographical, the territory he inhabits turns out, a little oddly, to be close to Larkin's:

Above a stretch of still unravaged weald
In our Black Country, in a cedar-shade,
I found, shared out in tennis-courts, a field
Where children of the local magnates played.

(*Collected Poems*, p. 15)

This, and the poem's conclusion ('But theirs is all the youth we might have had'), has more than a little in common, in theme and attitude, with Larkin's 'I Remember, I Remember'.

The weaknesses of *Brides of Reason* look as if they spring from a lack of confidence. *A Winter Talent*, Davie's second collection, opens by contrast with a marvellously assured poem, 'Time Passing, Beloved':

Time passing, and the memories of love
Coming back to me, carissima, no more mockingly
Than ever before; time passing, unslackening,
Unhastening, steadily; and no more
Bitterly, beloved, the memories of love
Coming into the shore.

How will it end? Time passing and our passages of love
As ever, beloved, blind
As ever before; time binding, unbinding
About us; and yet to remember
Never less chastening, nor the flame of love
Less like an ember.

What will become of us? Time
Passing, beloved, and we in a sealed
Assurance, unassailed
By memory. How can it end,
This siege of a shore that no misgivings have steeled,
No doubts defend?

(*Collected Poems*, p. 35)

This haunting piece is perhaps the most surprising poem in Davie's published work. It sets the precedent for his many subsequent changes of poetic style (which are therefore the less surprising) and it represents a radical development away from *Brides of Reason*. Equally, it does not subscribe to the 'manifesto' of *Purity of Diction in English Verse*. And clearly, the major change is in the syntactical structure of the poem: this is not the work of 'A pasticheur of late-Augustan styles' who insisted upon the straightforward syntax of prose. But it is the work of the man who published *Articulate Energy* two years earlier, and specifically of the man who wrote enthusiastically in that book of Susanne Langer and 'syntax as music':

> What distinguishes Mrs Langer's from all these other accounts of the poetry-music relationship is her insistence on music as pre-eminently articulation. In her view a poem is like a piece of music in that it articulates itself; and in thus establishing internal relations, establishes also relations of feeling, building up the structure, the morphology of feeling, and telling us 'what it feels like to feel'. In other words, the central act, of poetry as of music, is the creation of syntax, of meaningful arrangement. And hence (this seems to me the most salutary implication) the unit of poetry is not the 'passage', but *the poem*.
>
> (Articulate Energy, 1955, p. 19)

This is very much to the point: the unit of 'Time Passing, Beloved' is 'the poem' in exactly this sense. The poem's flow is only slightly and precisely disturbed by the three unanswered, unanswerable questions: 'How will it end?'; 'What will become of us?'; 'How can it end...?'. And the syntactical differences between this and Davie's earlier poems produce a change of tone as profound as the change which takes place in Gunn's poetry between, say, 'Lines for a Book' and 'My Sad Captains'. Though their methods are dissimilar, the effect in each case is of a shift from an aggressive tone (however defensive the impetus) to a seductive one, to return once more to Dodsworth's terms for Gunn. It is therefore interesting that Gunn should have contributed an extremely sensitive review of *A Winter Talent* to the magazine *Listen* at a time when he may well have been working on the poems in *My Sad Captains*:

> He [Davie] is concerned with style in the most important sense—i.e. as an instrument for the examination of experience. The poems are related by their all being part of the same exploration undertaken by the same man: an exploration and at the same time a definition of values. Even the slighter and less successful poems are worth careful reading in this context. The world is his, but it is worth understanding so that we may understand our own better.
>
> (Thom Gunn, 'Three Poets',
Listen, III:1, Winter 1958, p. 22)

Above all, in 'Time Passing, Beloved', Davie manages to judge his cadences with that exquisite precision which distinguishes some of his later poems (I have in mind particularly the *Essex Poems*, to which I shall return).

Nevertheless, 'Time Passing, Beloved' remains something of an oddity in *A Winter Talent:* elsewhere in the collection, Davie tends to retain his metrical and syntactical norms. Yet the earlier spiky allusiveness has mellowed, particularly in the descriptive poems ('The Wind at Penistone' is a fine example), and as Davie himself seems to admit in 'Heigh-ho on a Winter Afternoon':

> Yes I have 'mellowed', as you said I would,
> And that's a heigh-ho too for any man;
> Heigh-ho that means we fall short of alas
> Which sprigs the grave of higher hopes than ours.

(Collected Poems, p. 66)

This is a very English poem, in an almost self-parodying way:

> There is a heigh-ho in these glowing coals
> By which I sit wrapped in my overcoat
> As if for a portrait by Whistler. And there is
> A heigh-ho in the bird that noiselessly
> Flew just now past my window, to alight
> On winter's moulding, snow; and an alas,
> A heigh-ho and a desultory chip,
> Chip, chip on stone from somewhere down below.

What Davie has achieved here is a fusion of the syntax of prose with the music of 'Time Passing, Beloved'. The poem is rescued from nostalgic sentimentality partly by the syntactical elegance, partly by the familiar controlling irony: the poet makes his own self-consciousness clear within the first three lines of the poem ('As if for a portrait by Whistler': does this turn the poet into Thomas Carlyle?). Consequently, the reader's response to the final stanza is likely to be ambivalent (especially if he has the benefit of hindsight):

> What should we do to rate the long alas
> But skeeter down a steeper gradient?
> And then some falls are still more fortunate,
> The meteors spent, the tragic heroes stunned
> Who go out like a light. But here the chip,
> Chip, chip will flake the stone by slow degrees,
> For hour on hour the fire will gutter down,
> The bird will call at longer intervals.

Evocative and effective though this may be on one level, it is hard not to feel that the mellow vision is one which must inevitably be rejected by a writer as restless as Davie.

2

In fact, Davie chose to move on, as he often does, in two distinct complementary or contradictory directions. One impetus produced *The Forests of Lithuania*, his adaptations of Mickiewicz's *Pan Tadeusz*, which was published in 1959, indicating Davie's growing need to look elsewhere than England for his material and to look for new vantage points from which to view England. The other—and for the purposes of my argument here the more interesting—development resulted in a note written on 21 July 1957 and a remarkable poem, 'With the Grain', which Davie completed three days later. He rightly describes the note as 'a vulnerable piece of writing' but he reproduces it nevertheless in his *Collected Poems*. He describes his predicament in the first three paragraphs:

It is true that I am not a poet by nature, only by inclination; for my mind moves most easily and happily among abstractions, it relates ideas far more readily than it relates experiences. I have little appetite, only profound admiration, for sensuous fullness and immediacy; I have not the poet's need of concreteness. I have resisted this admission for so long, chiefly because a natural poet was above all what I wanted to be, but partly because I mistook my English empiricism for the poet's concreteness, and so thought my mind was unphilosophical whereas it is philosophical but in a peculiarly English way.

Most of the poems I have written are not natural poems, in one sense not truly poems, simply because the thought in them could have been expressed—at whatever cost in terseness and point—in a non-poetic way. This does not mean however that they are worthless, or that they are shams; for as much can be said of much of the poetry of the past that by common consent is worth reading and remembering. Nevertheless I have taken a decision to write no more poems of this kind, only poems which are, if not *naturally*, at all events *truly* poems throughout.

For a true poem can be written by a mind not naturally poetic—though by the inhuman labour of thwarting at every point the natural grain and bent. This working against the grain does not damage the mind, nor is it foolish; on the contrary, only by doing this does each true poem as it is written become an authentic widening of experience—a truth won from life against all odds, because a truth in and about a mode of experience to which the mind is normally closed.

(*Collected Poems*, p. 301)[3]

This is a very odd piece of writing, and one might be forgiven for wishing that Davie had left it unpublished. One has to assume, I think, that he is using the word 'poet' in a special, restricted (and unusually Leavisite) way: for major poets have often seemed to have minds which move 'most easily and happily among abstractions' and this applies to writers of very different periods and styles—Greville and Coleridge, for example. Even Yeats praises abstraction in some of his most famous lines:

The abstract joy,
The half-read wisdom of daemonic images,
Suffice the ageing man as once the growing boy.

(W. B. Yeats, *Collected Poems*, 1950, p. 232)

Were these minds not 'naturally poetic'? Apparently not. We know that

Yeats, for instance, produced thorough prose drafts of his poems; but Davie tells us that if the thought in a poem 'could have been expressed—at whatever cost in terseness and point—in a non-poetic way' then that work is not 'truly' a poem. Fortunately, Davie creates a sizeable loophole in his third paragraph, and indeed very nearly manages to imply that the writing of poems by 'a mind not naturally poetic' is in fact a more noble, difficult, and exciting enterprise than the work of the 'natural poet'.

I remarked that there is in *Brides of Reason* a feeling of defensiveness which recurs in Davie's work; and I think that this curious note, and his stylistic restlessness, spring from the same causes. The lack of confidence which so often (and at times so unhelpfully) appears in his occasional prose has brought with it a receptiveness, a possibly naive readiness to be converted to new poetic programmes, each of which will be more truthful or more fulfilling than what has gone before. And so this note quite openly stands the creed of the Movement on its head: the voice which informs it is Pound's. As Bernard Bergonzi says (not of this note but of Davie's writing in the late fifties and early sixties in general), 'one can only conclude that he had succumbed to the strange magnetic attraction that symbolism has for those who attempt to study it in a spirit of detachment or even suspicion' (*Critical Quarterly*, IV:4, Winter 1962, p. 297).

All this might suggest that 'With the Grain' ought to be an unsuccessful or unconfident poem, or at least a radical departure from Davie's earlier work. In fact, it is a development both of the 'sculptural' ideas of 'Heigh-ho on a Winter Afternoon' and of the musical syntax of 'Time Passing, Beloved':

> Why, by an ingrained habit, elevate
>   Into their own ideas
> Activities like carpentry, become
>   The metaphors of graining?
> Gardening, the one word, tilth? Or thought,
>   The idea of having ideas,
> Resolved into images of tilth and graining?
> An ingrained habit . . . This is fanciful:
>   And there's the rub
> Bristling, where the irritable block
>   Screams underneath the blade
> Of love's demand, or in crimped and gouged-out
>   Shavings only, looses
> Under a peeling logic its perceptions.
> Language (mine, when wounding,
>   Yours, back-biting) lacks
> No whorl nor one-way shelving. It resists,
>   Screams its remonstrance, planes

Reluctantly to a level. And the most
  Reasonable of settlements betrays
Unsmoothed resentment under the caress.
                        (Collected Poems, p. 109)

This is the first section of the poem, which Davie himself describes as
'obscure'. I find it relatively clear, especially in comparison with some of
his later work. Where it differs from the earlier poems and from the
precepts of *Purity of Diction in English Verse* is in its use of (and indeed
discussion of) metaphor, which is the subject of much of the poem. It is a
deliberate and very eloquent recantation and much else besides; hence, at
the beginning of the second section, Davie takes the prized notion of
purity and shows how it may be transformed into something else. And,
appropriately, he does so metaphorically, setting up now an analogy
between poetry and painting:

The purest hue, let only the light be sufficient
  Turns colour. And I was told
If painters frequent St Ives
  It is because the light
There, under the cliff, is merciful. I dream
  Of an equable light upon words
And as painters paint in St Ives, the poets speaking.

Under that cliff we should say, my dear,
  Not what we mean, but what
The words would mean. We should speak,
  As carpenters work,
With the grain of our words. We should utter
  Unceasingly the hue of love
Safe from the battery of changeable light.

The crucial difference is between 'hue' and 'colour': hue, one assumes,
indicates something sensitive and subdued, colour something richer but
also more brash. If one is to translate these terms of painting into terms of
poetry, one's instinct is to return to *Purity of Diction in English Verse* and
to equate 'hue' with 'chaste' language and 'colour' with 'hyperbolical and
highly metaphorical language' (*Purity of Diction in English Verse*, p. 18).
But this won't quite meet the case, for Davie has apparently been
persuaded by symbolism that language can be at once sparse and meta-
phorical (see the comments on *Essex Poems* and particularly on 'Ezra
Pound in Pisa' below).

There are other fine and interesting distinctions here: 'Not what we
mean, but what/The words would mean', words seen as a solid raw
material, like stone or wood, an idea reinforced by the pun on 'would'. Yet
surely the most astonishing quality of this part of the poem is the
synthesis of a complex and condensed literary argument with an
emotional intensity which is reminiscent of 'Time Passing, Beloved'. The

poem seems to shape and to define itself (in deference to Davie's note, I resist the word 'naturally') so that by the end of the third section the argument has grown to a conclusion more optimistic and more just than anything in the related note:

And will the poet, carpenter of light,
    Work with the grain henceforward?
If glitterings won't fetch him
    Nor the refractory crystal,
Will he never again look into the source of light
    Aquiline, but fly
Always out of the sun, unseen till softly alighting?
Why, by an ingrained habit, elevate
    Into the light of ideas
The colourful trades, if not like Icarus
    To climb the beam? High lights
Are always white, but this ideal sun
    Dyes only more intensely, and we find
Enough cross-graining in the most abstract nature.

In one sense, at the level of argument, the problems of the poem may not have been fully resolved: but the more important resolution is embodied in the fact that the poem exists. It seems to me to be one of the most fascinating and accomplished poems written by Davie, or by anyone else, in the last thirty years.

Davie spent the academic year 1957-8 in the USA. 'Unlikely as it may seem,' he says, *A Sequence for Francis Parkman* 'represents my response to North America on my first visit' (*Collected Poems*, p. 303). George Hartley, the editor of *Listen*, recorded Davie reading the sequence in Cambridge in 1960 and published the text and the recording together in 1961. Certainly, it is surprisingly rhetorical: but the rhetoric is carefully undercut by the clipped, cryptic prose comments which precede each poem. 'Montcalm' ('He died before he could learn which of his children had pre-deceased him,' Davie explains) is the most obviously rhetorical of the poems, yet it has its own dryness:

Both earned their stucco. Marble was reserved
To honour the intrepid, the serene
And the successful Amherst. But it served,
Pompous and frigid as it was, the phrase
'A martial glory': common ground between
The public lives, the private, Kent, Quebec,
And Candiac by Nîmes in Languedoc.

(*Collected Poems*, p. 124)

The poem—and especially the carefully balanced counterpoint of the penultimate line—comes over particularly well in Davie's admirable reading of it (it is worth obtaining the original 1961 publication of *A*

Sequence for Francis Parkman, since the recording is obviously not included with the *Collected Poems).*

The other point to be made about the *Parkman* sequence is that it embodies not only a concern with history but also a new awareness of geographical scope and of the differences between Englishness and Americanness. In the 'Letter to Curtis Bradford' which stands as a coda to the sequence, Davie writes:

> ... I only guess,
> I guess at it out of my Englishness
> And envy you out of England. Man with man
> Is all our history; American,
> You met with spirits. Neither white nor red
> The melancholy, disinherited
> Spirit of mid-America, but this,
> The manifested copiousness, the bounties.
>
> *(Collected Poems,* p. 128)

Taken together with the dense texture of 'With the Grain', these two poems seem in retrospect to signpost Davie's second and more permanent visit to America and his championing of Olson and Dorn with their use of 'The manifested copiousness, the bounties'.

3

Davie's next collection, *Events and Wisdoms,* is a curiously hybrid book: the poems in it were originally grouped in four sections of unexplained and not immediately evident significance, prefaced by 'Two Dedications'; in his *Collected Poems,* Davie has jettisoned the sectional divisions and retained the 'Dedications'. One of these, 'Barnsley Cricket Club', is a fine example of his most assured 'English' manner; we are not told where it was written, but since Davie refers to 'This layabout July in another climate' and another poem in the collection is called 'New York in August' it may well have been written in America. Seldom has the 'Englishness' of which Davie speaks in 'A Letter to Curtis Bradford' been more tellingly or concisely expressed:

> 'A thing worth doing is worth doing well,'
> Says Shaw Lane Cricket Ground
> Between the showers of a July evening,
> As the catch is held and staid hand-clappings swell.
>
> *(Collected Poems,* p. 134)

There is here and in other poems in *Events and Wisdoms* a growing tension between Englishness and Americanness; thus, at the end of 'Barnsley Cricket Club', Davie writes:

> How soon the shadows fall, how soon and long!
> The score-board stretches to a grandson's feet.

This layabout July in another climate
Ought not to prove firm turf, well-tended, wrong.

The force of that word *ought* is crucial. On the one hand, there is Davie's profound affection for England, an affection charged with the accuracy of unsentimental reminiscence ('Barnsley and District'):

Judy Sugden! Judy, I made you caper
With rage when I said the British Fascist
Sheet your father sold was a jolly good paper

And you had agreed and I said, Yes, it holds
Vinegar, and everyone laughed and imagined
The feel of fish and chips warm in its folds.

(Collected Poems, p. 152)

The very English diction and English cliché ('jolly good paper'; 'A thing worth doing is worth doing well') belie the ironist's defensive postures which creep into the poems. On the other hand, Davie is well able to move into an entirely American diction and vocabulary:

At Ventucopa, elevation
Two-eight-nine-six, the water hydrant frozen,
Deserted or broken settlements,
Gasoline stations closed and boarded.

(Collected Poems, p. 148)

The Americanisms of these lines, from 'In California', are plainly deliberate, self-conscious, and extreme. Nevertheless, one must stress that the usages of 'elevation', 'Two-eight-nine-six', 'hydrant', 'broken', 'settlements', and 'Gasoline' in this short stanza would all be uncolloquial if not incomprehensible in Barnsley. One would begin to suspect Davie of a kind of literary ventriloquism were it not for the plentiful evidence that this English/American crisis is so deeply felt. It becomes clear in Davie's subsequent work that his quarrel is not with proletarian England but with literary England, so that changes in attitude may be expressed appropriately in changes of literary style. In the final poem of *Events and Wisdoms*, 'The Hardness of Light' (an interesting title when set against the second stanza of 'With the Grain'), Davie looks back and, with his fondness for literary manifestos, forward:

'Via Portello,' I wrote,
'The fruity garbage-heaps . . .'
As if someone had read my poems,
Padua eight years later
Is so hot no one sleeps.

But this is a different quarter,
Just off the *autostrada*,
Touched by that wand of transit,
Californian, hopeful . . .
I grow older, harder.

(Collected Poems, p. 163)

The last two lines could hardly be more accurately predictive.

I must note two other developments in *Events and Wisdoms,* neither of them central to my argument. One is the inclusion of a few poems of baffling opacity, notably 'Right Wing Sympathies': the true literary ancestor of this poem, with its short stanzas, apparently ordinary syntax, and impenetrable meanings, seems to be Eliot's 'A Cooking Egg'. The other development is most clearly evident in the moving sequence of poems, 'After an Accident'. This is certainly an unusually personal piece of writing for Davie, and it prompted the American critic M. L. Rosenthal, in the course of an otherwise sketchy and superficial comment on Davie's work, to write as follows:

> Thus, Davie has in *Events and Wisdoms* begun not only to ponder Concrete but to use the confessional mode in a perfectly natural way. 'Wide France' and 'Across the Way' are poems of family turbulence, and the sequence 'After an Accident' (about the effects of a terrible automobile smashup in which Davie was involved) is a serious effort to repossess a psychological state that was both traumatic and productive of painful private realisations.
>
> (M. L. Rosenthal, *The New Poets,* 1967, p. 210)

It is not clear to me why anyone, least of all a literary critic, should suppose that 'the confessional mode' is in any way a guarantee of quality in a poem, but this remark may serve to remind us that such suppositions were widely held during the mid-sixties and that *Events and Wisdoms* appeared in the year after Sylvia Plath's death. The humour of pondering Concrete seems to elude Rosenthal. The passage is typical of his perverse and inaccurate chapter on 'Contemporary British Poetry' in *The New Poets.*

It is 'The Hardness of Light' which anticipates *Essex Poems* most clearly. These poems seem to me to most nearly achieve a synthesis of Davie's poetic programmes to date: they have the precision of the Movement without the coyness; less expansive than the *Parkman* sequence, they possess nevertheless a pared-down rhetoric; and some of them manage to work symbolic forcefulness into a sparse texture. And there is the familiar reflexiveness, the poems which are at least partly about writing poetry:

I smell a smell of death.
Roethke, who died last year
with whom I drank in London,
wrote the book I am reading;
a friend, of a firm mind,
has died or is dying now,
a telegram informs me;
the wife of a neighbour died
in three quick months of cancer.
Love and art I practise;

they seem to be worth no more
and no less than they were.
The firm mind practised neither.
It practised charity
vocationally and
yet for the most part truly.
Roethke, who practised both,
was slack in his art by the end.

The practice of an art
is to convert all terms
into the terms of art.
By the end of the third stanza
death is a smell no longer;
it is a problem of style.
A man who ought to know me
wrote in a review
my emotional life was meagre.

(*Collected Poems*, pp. 182-3)

That is the whole of 'July, 1964'. In an obvious sense, it is a modest poem, quiet and concise; but in other and more interesting ways, it is very ambitious. The weight borne by the three repeated abstractions—death, practice, art—is immense; each is made concrete in a number of different contexts, without strain. The metre (which looks like syllabic sevens—a form only rarely used by Davie, unlike Gunn—but isn't) is firmly but subtly controlled. The poem convincingly proves its own hypothesis, for death *has* become 'a problem of style' by the third stanza, and operates as an ironic piece of literary criticism: it is controlled and precise, and pure in diction, in exactly the areas where Roethke's last poems are 'slack'. The distinction between 'vocationally' and 'truly' reminds us of the distinctions in the 1957 note quoted earlier; and the conclusion is evidence, to be reinforced later by 'To Certain English Poets', of Davie's disenchantment with English literary life.

'July, 1964' is, like 'With the Grain', very much a product of the working poet, the poet as carpenter. It seems right to speak of these poems as being pared-down, chiselled-down; particularly 'Ezra Pound in Pisa':

Excellence is sparse.
I am made of a Japanese mind
Concerning excellence:
However sparred or fierce
The furzy elements,
Let them be but few
And spaciously dispersed,
And excellence appears.

(*Collected Poems*, p. 188)

The sparseness is effective not only in giving to Davie's arguments a new hard-edged clarity and directness; it is also appropriate to the descriptive pieces dealing with the bleak beauty of East Anglia. 'Sunburst' is a fine example which reaffirms Davie's concern with light:

> The light wheels and comes in
> over the seawall
> and the bitten turf
> that not only wind has scathed but
> all this wheeling and flashing, this
> sunburst comes across us.

(Collected Poems, p. 186)

The sense of flow and of cadence from 'Time Passing, Beloved' reappears here too. But despite the beauty of some of the descriptive writing in *Essex Poems,* Davie's restlessness, his sense of the limitations of English-ness, is much in evidence.[4] 'Thanks to Industrial Essex' provides one explanation:

> Landscapes of supertax
> Record a dreadful failure
> As clearly as the lack
> Of a grand or expansively human
> Scale to the buildings of Ilford.
>
> The scale of that deprivation
> Goes down in no statistics.

(Collected Poems, p. 191)

Other explanations are to be found in the group of poems written at the same time which Davie has added to his *Collected Poems* under the title 'More Essex Poems'. Here the bitterness is harsher, and often a good deal less eloquent. In 'New Year Wishes for the English' (1966) Davie is in control, but only just:

> May you have, against the incessant
> Rain of the new, the all-new,
> Indifference as an umbrella.
>
> May you be quiet, may you
> Not be hectored by me,
> But left alone for a little.
>
> May you recognise that these
> Are wishes for the inception
> Of a long recuperation;
>
> That they are not what a poet
> Would wish if he could,
> But the most he dares to hope for.

(Collected Poems, p. 210)

The same impatience with 'the all-new' finds prose expression in the 1966

'Postscript' to *Purity of Diction in English Verse:*
    Yet in 1966 'style'—in clothes, in behaviour, in haircuts, in the theatre,
    in pop-music—is one thing that the self-regarding Britain of Carnaby
    Street is not short of. If I were now writing *Purity of Diction in English
    Verse* I should need to take greater pains than I did in 1952, to
    distinguish the literary styles I was analysing from what passes for
    style in the hectic circles that invest or exploit or tamely follow the
    dictates of the 'with it'.
                              (*Purity of Diction in English Verse*, p. 202)
And in 'To Certain English Poets', which I shall not quote at length, the
shaky control of 'New Year Wishes' disintegrates into mere rancour. It
opens, 'My dears, don't I know?' and concludes, 'will you, contained, still
burn with that surly pluck?' (*Collected Poems*, p. 211). 'Epistle. To
Enrique Caracciolo Trejo' conveys the dilemma more clearly and more
justly:
    A shrunken world
    Stares from my pages.
    What a pellet the authentic is!
    My world of poetry,
    Enrique, is not large.
    Day by day it is smaller.
    These poems that you have
    Given me, I might
    Have made them English once.
    Now they are inessential.
                                            (*Collected Poems*, p. 213)
Though 1966 represents, for good reasons, a peak in Davie's distaste for
Englishness, related concerns are clearly evident as early as 'Rejoinder to
a Critic' from *A Winter Talent* (*Collected Poems*, p. 65) and as recently as
Davie's Editorial in the second number of *PN Review* (*PN Review*, 2,
1977, pp. 1-2).
    At the end of *Essex Poems*, there are three poems collectively entitled
'From the New World': these Iowan landscapes seem the inevitable
extension of Davie's transatlantic yearnings and pared-down style in the
poems which have preceded them. The last poem of all is called 'Or,
Solitude' (which was Wordsworth's eventual subtitle to 'Lucy Gray', also
a poem about solitude and snow, an ironic contrast); it concludes:
    The metaphysicality
    Of poetry, how I need it!
    And yet it was for years
    What I refused to credit.
                                            (*Collected Poems*, p. 202)
This, interestingly, is the original version of this stanza as it appeared in
the *New Statesman* of 31 December 1965 and as it appears in the *Collected*

Poems. In the meantime, when the poem appeared in *Essex Poems,* Davie revised the first line to read, 'The transcendental nature . . .' (*Essex Poems,* 1969, p.53). Perhaps this was a more honest and accurate line; but the original and now restored version sounds better and is much the more rhythmically satisfying of the two in the context of the poem. So the 'problem of style' is not entirely solved.

'Or, Solitude' seems to me a remarkable poem, as important a landmark as 'Time Passing, Beloved' or 'With the Grain'. Karl Miller has written at some length about it, and I quote part of his enthusiastic analysis with which I wholeheartedly agree:

> 'Or, Solitude' is a beautiful and an engrossing poem. And there can be few more startling effects in modern poetry than the transition from a dreamy, incantatory Iowa to the bucking-bronco syllables with which the last stanza begins. Metaphor. Metaphysics. Magic. They are all present. And the surprise caused by the transition would seem to point to the presence of exigent feelings behind the varieties of argument and disagreement which I have been examining, despite their often calm and voluntary air. There's a sense of tension, fission, of an explosive volte-face. The poetry of statement appears to have been banished but—another of Davie's incongruities—it hurtles back at the transition and fills the remainder of the poem.
>
> (*Writing in England Today,* ed. Karl Miller, 1968, p. 23)

4

Many of Davie's more recent poems have been, for anyone who admires his clipped lyricism (less of a paradox than it might seem) and his assured way with a cadence in *Essex Poems,* perplexing or disappointing or both; yet when they perplex or disappoint they do so, curiously, in an honourable way, usually as the result of genuinely unresolved tensions. Michael Schmidt, reviewing the *Collected Poems,* has diagnosed the problem, I think rightly. Schmidt notes that the early poems 'presuppose a literary consensus and address themselves to it'. He adds:

> Recently he has been imagining (in the 'Epistles to Eva Hesse') a new consensus and addressing it, wittily persuading and admonishing it, with the knowledge that it does not yet exist, but that imagining may hurry it into being.
>
> (*Critical Quarterly,* XV:1, Spring 1973, p. 81)

A little later in his review, Schmidt gets to what I take to be the core of the problem:

> His early poems, and unfortunately a number of his most recent poems . . . continually refer to areas of fact or allusion not contained within, nor ultimately necessary to, the poem. In other words, the poem is not self-sufficient. It makes us readjust regularly to our own

jarring ignorance, to distracting surprises (like seeing Thom Gunn cycle up in one poem), to a mild sense of betrayal.

In reading the 'Epistles to Eva Hesse' and 'England' and some of the more recent uncollected poems, one is constantly struck by a deliberate refusal to explicate on the poet's part. Of course this is not new: Davie has at various times been a master of the unhelpful footnote in his criticism and has indeed published some incomprehensible poems in the past. But the extent and the obscurity of allusion, and the deliberation with which he refuses to be helpful in some recent poems, are new and disturbing. Two long poems at the end of the *Collected Poems*, 'Trevenen' and 'Vancouver', are provided with J. H. Prynne-like notes which would be of little use to anyone outside one of the copyright libraries.

'The scholar's pleasure is the poet's vice,' wrote Davie in a poem called 'The Poet-Scholar' (*Essays in Criticism*, V:1, 1955, p. 43) which he does not include in his *Collected Poems*, either because, as he claims, he has lost sight of some early poems in periodicals or because it gives the game away. Plainly, the poet-scholar dichotomy is one of Davie's most central and continuing unresolved tensions. 'The poet-scholar cannot keep apart/The gift and the investment': but in that case he fails to take account of the fact that poetry and scholarship require not necessarily different sorts of *reader* but different sorts of *reading*.

Graham Hough, in a passage which I discussed in my first chapter, insisted that 'The traditional poet, or any poet so far as he is traditional, addresses his readers in the confidence that he will be understood' (*Image and Experience*, p.40). Here is another unresolved tension, for Davie often lacks that confidence (he may, as Schmidt suggests, like to imagine it) though he definitely considers himself a traditional poet. On this point Davie is explicit: the crucial evidence is to be found in his poem 'Morning' (*Poetry Nation*, 1, 1973, p. 15) and the related 'A Comment' (*ibid.*, pp. 54-58). 'What I hope and think,' says Davie,

> is that my poem has form, and of a very traditional kind; because it belongs to a tradition of poems from many centuries in many languages, any one of which poems could be entitled 'A Description of the Morning'.

He goes on to relate his 'Morning' to John Cunningham's, and to Christopher Smart's 'A Morning Piece; or an hymn for the haymakers', adding that he has misquoted Smart's poem in his own.

> Now, I didn't quote so as to give a knowing nod to some in-group reader who could be expected to 'pick it up'; when I adapted Smart's verses into mine, I didn't have the reader in mind at all, but only my own pleasure. . . .

The poet's pleasure, or the scholar's? The question is unfair, even though it is provoked by Davie's own 'The Poet-Scholar'. It is a question evidently in Davie's mind, however, for he goes on in his next paragraph:

I'm supposed to be a learned poet, though compared with Milton (or Christopher Smart!) I'm a very *un*learned poet, and I write unlearned poetry. Still, I will plead guilty to having in the past used bits of out-of-the-way information that I happened to have, without paying enough attention to how a reader's lack of it might fox him. But it ought to be clear that this isn't that sort of case: *this* sort of knowledge, awareness of the genres, is something that a reader *must* have, and I have *every right* to expect it. Poetry has always fed upon its own past in this way, and if it ceases to do so now, it will change into something for which we'll have to find a new name. Impatient ignorance of the past is common now, and is tolerated by educators, who ought to know better; to speak for myself, it is this which gives me my direst fore-bodings about a future for poetry, my own or anyone else's.

There, precisely and in a form which ought to command universal assent in a civilised society, is a statement of the poet's legitimate demands on the 'common reader' and of the gap between those demands and contemporary (and future?) reality. Davie is right to imply a distinction between the learned poet (the author of 'Trevenen' perhaps) and the informed poet (the author of 'Morning'): the former, which Davie has been too often, assumes specialised knowledge which the ordinary reader of poetry is unlikely to possess, whereas the latter doesn't.

The trouble is that it is when Davie loses the 'essential confidence that he will be understood' that he takes refuge in defensive obscurity. I admire the 'Epistles to Eva Hesse' for their virtuosity and because they prove the continuing vitality of a tight metrical and rhyme scheme; but elsewhere, and especially in 'England', the reluctance to communicate, to go even a quarter of the way to meet the reader, seems largely to invalidate the poetic achievement. And this is not a matter of poetic style or necessarily of difficulty, but a matter of tone.

Let me be specific and take two allusive poems, one an early piece, the other much more recent. The first is 'The Fountain':

Feathers up fast, and steeples; then in clods
Thuds into its first basin; thence as surf
Smokes up and hangs; irregularly slops
Into its second, tattered like a shawl;
There, chill as rain, stipples a danker green,
Where urgent tritons lob their heavy jets.

For Berkeley this was human thought, that mounts
From bland assumptions to inquiring skies,
There glints with wit, fumes into fancies, plays
With its negations, and at last descends,
As by a law of nature, to its bowl
Of thus enlightened but still common sense.

We who have no such confidence must gaze

With all the more affection on these forms,
These spires, these plumes, these calm reflections, these
Similitudes of surf and turf and shawl,
Graceful returns upon acceptances.
We ask of fountains only that they play,
Though that was not what Berkeley meant at all.

(*Collected Poems*, pp. 59-60)

'We who have no such confidence . . .' indeed: the poem touches on that very issue, that very word. But this engaging piece of writing works elegantly on a number of levels, one of which is literal description: it appeals to our 'enlightened but still common sense' but it could be enjoyed even if we had never heard of Bishop Berkeley[5]—just as 'Morning' could be enjoyed even if we had never heard of Christopher Smart. Although 'The Fountain' has a few hints of awkwardness, it seems to have confidence in its craftsmanship and confidence in its readers. Consider by contrast 'Robinson Jeffers at Point Sur':

Nature? No, not Nature.
What did she ever make
Here but an artless moan
Of ecstasy some feature
Of coast must, for the sake
Of Art, blush for, and own?
So much is lacking!
Much (O pioneers)
A waggon-train's supplies
Won't run to. There is no
Substitute, it appears:
A long past fructifies.

So much is lacking! So
Much that we have is a mess:
Joaquin Miller, Bret
Harte and—years ago—
Alfred Noyes in distress
Lest (Kipling's) we forget

The Mission bells! Not that,
Not that at all events!
Colonialist mistakes,
Well-meant, pound into fat
Kiwanis' prose our sense
For what, here builds and makes.

(*The Listener*, 1 March 1973)

Here, it seems to me, the allusions and the compressions of syntax are thrown at the reader spitefully: make what you can of that! And here, as in

'England', even the informed reader may well be thrown by his own 'jarring ignorance' and have to break off and unravel, so that any fluency which the poem might have is undermined. A number of particularly impatient, bad-tempered poems (e.g. 'Berryman', *Times Literary Supplement*, 29 June 1973, and 'An End to Good Humour', *The Listener*, 18 October 1973) appear to date from the period of the famous row with Larkin over *The Oxford Book of Twentieth Century English Verse*, to which I shall return; there may be a connection here. Davie claims that 'poems are fun to write, and should be fun to read; pleasure is what we're talking about' (*Poetry Nation*, 1, 1973, p. 55): but there are points in his work where one doubts this.

Then there is Englishness and Americanness. Englishness continues to haunt him: 'We really *are* a small nation, aren't we?' (*Poetry Nation*, 2, 1974, p. 80). If there is such a thing as an English literary tradition, and if it is a thing of intellectual and cultural substance, then Davie is probably the major poet of our time most committed to it: he is far more committed to it than Larkin, for instance, whose apparent Englishness so often turns out to be a species of quaintness. Both *Thomas Hardy and British Poetry* and *The Shires* are homages to England (and so, of course, are Davie's angriest outbursts at philistinism and ignorance homages to 'the England of Fulke Greville as well as the England of Shakespeare, the Dissenters' England of Isaac Watts as well as the Romish England of Alexander Pope and the Anglican England of Jonathan Swift, the would-be republican England of Walter Savage Landor as well as the monarchical England of Alfred Tennyson [*PN Review*, 2, 1977, p. 2]). As a poetic project, *The Shires* seems from the outset unlikely to succeed: it resembles Gunn's *Positives* as an oddity, a well-produced illustrated book of poems on a predetermined theme. *The Shires* was published in 1974 and, in view of the poems published in 1973 which I have just mentioned, it is hardly surprising to find that many of the pieces in *The Shires* are off-hand and perfunctory. But against throwaway jottings such as 'Staffordshire' one can set beautifully realised poems such as 'Cheshire':

> A lift to the spirit, when everything fell into place!
> So that was what those ruined towers remained from:
> Engine-houses, mills. Our Pennine crests
> Had not been always mere unfettered space.
>
> (The Shires, 1974, unnumbered pages)

The reader certainly experiences a lift to the spirit when Davie writes as well as this. Elegiac and affectionate yet unsentimental, the fourth and final stanza unites the finest qualities of poems as different as 'Barnsley Cricket Club' and 'July, 1964':

> And Mr Auden, whom I never knew,
> Is dead in Vienna. A post-industrial landscape

He celebrated often, and expounded
How it can bleakly solace. And that's true.

The publication (before this appears in print) of Davie's new collection of poems, *In the Stopping Train,* and his *The Poet in the Imaginary Museum: Essays of Two Decades* will no doubt suggest new perspectives and directions; considering his literary career so far, it would be astonishing if they didn't. Alan Hurd writes to me: 'And as for D. Davie: how *do* you take aim at such a fast-moving target?' I shall evade the question by suggesting that there are in fact several Donald Davies. One is the learned but often hostile and uncommunicative author of 'Right-Wing Sympathies' and 'England'. The second can be angry and abrupt ('New Year Wishes for the English', 'To Certain English Poets') but is at best the most concerned and committed critic of contemporary Englishness. And the third is the author of 'Time Passing, Beloved', 'With the Grain', 'Or, Solitude', and at least as many eloquent, engrossing poems as any English poet of our time, a major poet if not (in deference to yet another Davie) a natural one. And that's true.

NOTES

1. See also: 'A New Aestheticism? A. Alvarez talks to Donald Davie', *The Modern Poet,* ed. Ian Hamilton, 1968, pp. 157-176.
2. In earlier publications of this poem, the penultimate line of the quoted section reads: 'To find the stance impressive and absurd'. In 'England', Davie provides a characteristic recantation:

> A neutral
> tone was (Note the passive
> voice) preferred by no one
> really, no one at all.
>
> *(Collected Poems,* p. 224)

3. For a consideration of the differences between poetry as 'a special kind of discourse' and poetry as 'a special kind of art', see Davie's broadcast talk, 'Two Analogies for Poetry' in *The Listener,* 5 April 1962.
4. A major factor in Davie's restlessness at this time was his experience as Professor of English and Pro-Vice-Chancellor at the University of Essex. The nature of that experience is reflected in a number of these poems; in a series of 'Views' articles contributed to *The Listener* (21 March, 11 April, 4 July 1968); and perhaps most strikingly in Donald Wesling's letter to *The Listener* of 18 July 1968. But Davie had suspected much earlier 'that England is a country where even the poets are philistines without knowing it' *(Poetry,* Chicago, 100:2, May 1962, p. 123), an opinion which is very close to his 'New Year Wishes for the English' and which is repeated in his broadcast, 'The Failure of a Dialogue': 'In Britain, the philistine is usually very humane: he thinks that "the poetry is in the

pity," and the British poet agrees with him, thus offering the extra-ordinary spectacle of poet and philistine combined in one person' *(The Listener,* 27 August 1970). He has returned to this line of argument more recently, notably in 'A Comment', *Poetry Nation,* 1, 1973, pp. 54-58; 'The Varsity Match', *Poetry Nation,* 2, 1974, pp. 72-80; and 'Editorial', *PN Review,* 2, 1977, pp. 1-2.

5. About whom Davie has written extensively. See, e.g., 'Berkeley and the Style of Dialogue' in *The English Mind: Studies in the English Moralists presented to Basil Willey,* ed. Hugh Sykes Davies and George Watson, Cambridge, 1964, pp. 90-196.

Chapter Four

PHILIP LARKIN: AN UNCLE SHOUTING SMUT

1

It is probably fair to say that Philip Larkin is less highly regarded within academic circles than either Thom Gunn or Donald Davie but much more widely read (and understood) than either Gunn or Davie outside them. Davie describes Larkin as 'the best-loved poet of his generation' (*The Listener*, 29 March 1973); while Anthony Thwaite writes, 'In a straightforward Wordsworthian sense, he is a man speaking to men (though his detractors might put it that he is too often simply a chap chatting to chaps' (*The Survival of Poetry*, ed. Martin Dodsworth, 1970, p. 37). But although Larkin's work, no less than Gunn's or Davie's, demonstrates the vitality and flexibility of traditional structures in contemporary English poetry, critical opinion of him has become sharply divided since the publication of *The Oxford Book of Twentieth Century English Verse*, which he edited, in 1973, and his most recent collection of poems, *High Windows*, in 1974.

Larkin's first book of poems, *The North Ship*, was published in 1945 and reissued, with an autobiographical introduction by the poet, in 1966. Those early poems lean heavily upon Yeats: Larkin tells us that he 'used to limber up by turning the pages of the 1933 plum-coloured Macmillan edition, which stopped at "Words for Music Perhaps", and which meant that I never absorbed the harsher last poems' (Introduction to *The North Ship*, 1966, p. 10). He adds that in 1946 he discovered Hardy, and that 'When the reaction came, it was undramatic, complete and permanent.' Like the equally entertaining introduction to the reissue of his first novel, *Jill*, this needs to be approached as reminiscence and not as literary criticism: the influence of Yeats was certainly there, 'pervasive as garlic,' as Larkin says (*The North Ship*, p.9), but we should not be persuaded that after 1946 he became 'a very Hardyesque poet' and that all traces of Yeats disappeared instantly and irrevocably from his work.[1] In *The North Ship*, according to Larkin, 'I don't think I had anything serious to write about ... or at least if I had I couldn't see it' (Interview in *Tracks*, 1, 1967, p.7); so the collection is inevitably derivative. Certainly, a 'reaction' took place in 1946 or 1947, but I suggest that it was less a matter of Larkin discovering Hardy than of Larkin discovering himself: about this time, after publishing two very impressive novels (*Jill* and *A Girl in Winter*, though biographical notes about Larkin as late as the mid-fifties mention only one novel, and Faber's mis-dating of *A Girl in Winter* —1957 for 1947—in at least one printing complicates matters still further), he stopped writing prose fiction. 'When I stopped writing novels,' he said in the interview already quoted, 'it was a great disappointment to me: I went on trying in the 1945-50 period' (*ibid.*, p. 9). As the novelist dried up, the poet found his mature style: 'Waiting for Breakfast' dates from 1946 and so does 'Wedding-Wind', Anthony Thwaite tells us, adding, 'from now on the personality is an achieved and consistent one, each poem re-stating or adding another facet to what has gone before' (*The Survival of Poetry*, p. 45). Both these poems were included in the privately-printed *XX Poems* of 1951—a collection which, like one of the novels, has been invisible in some biographical and bibliographical accounts of Larkin.

XX Poems, however, has become invisible in other ways too: the edition was of one hundred copies and it has not been reprinted. Peter Ferguson (in *Agenda*, 14:3, 1976, pp. 53-65) calls it, with some justification, 'The Missing Link'; and the following table, which shows the overlaps with *The Less Deceived* and (in one case) with the second edition of *The North Ship*, will suggest both its pivotal position and the interestingly unchronological arrangement of *The Less Deceived*:

I	'Wedding-wind'	*LD*, p.15.
II	'Modesties'	
III	"Always too eager for the future, we ..."*LD*, p.20, as 'Next, Please'	
IV	"Even so distant, I can taste the grief ..."*LD*, p.27, as 'Deceptions'	
V	"Latest face, so effortless ..."*LD*, p.41, as 'Latest Face'	
VI	'Arrival'	
VII	"Since the majority of me ..."	
VIII	'Spring'	*LD*, p.36.
IX	"Waiting for breakfast, while she brushed her hair ..."	
		NS (1966), p.48, as XXXII
X	'Two Portraits of Sex: (1) Oils'	
XI	'Two Portraits of Sex: (2) Etching'	*LD*, p.19, as 'Dry-Point'
XII	"On longer evenings ..."*LD*, p.17, as 'Coming'	
XIII	"Since we agreed to let the road between us ..."	
		LD, p.26, as 'No Road'
XIV	"If my darling were once to decide ..."*LD*, p.42, as 'If, My Darling'	
XV	"Who called love conquering ..."	
XVI	'The widest prairies have electric fences ..."	
		LD, p.27, as 'Wires'
XVII	'The Dedicated'	
XVIII	'Wants'	*LD*, p.22.
XIX	"There is an evening coming in ..."*LD*, p.21, as 'Going'	
XX	'At Grass'	*LD*, p.45.

One is struck by the way in which the poem which was to provide the title for *The Less Deceived* appears so early (IV) in *XX Poems;* and also by the unnerving way in which some of the untitled pieces in *XX Poems* shed their 'early', *North Ship*-like appearance and become decisively products of the mature Larkin when they are given characteristic titles in *The Less Deceived*. Most of the excluded poems are slight (though not as slight as some in *The North Ship*) and one—the first of the 'Two Portraits of Sex'—is quite extraordinarily clumsy. The two exceptions are VI ('Arrival') and VII.

 The first of these describes the author's arrival in a 'new city' in terms which seem clearly to foreshadow later poems: morning is 'a glass door', windows 'flock open', the past 'dries in a wind'; and in the second stanza Larkin asks,

> Now let me lie down, under
> A wide-branched indifference.

But the most interesting effect comes, as so often in Larkin, at the end of the final stanza where a typical congestion resolves into an equally typical bleak clarity:

> For this ignorance of me
> Seems a kind of innocence.
> Fast enough I shall wound it:
> Let me breathe till then
> Its milk-aired Eden,
> Till my own life impound it—
> Slow-falling; grey-veil-hung; a theft,
> A style of dying only.

> *(XX Poems,* 1951, unnumbered pages)

Despite the slackness of the verse, that is a very familiar kind of Larkin conclusion; and so, from VII, is this:

> A silence of minorities
> That, unopposed at last, return
> Each night with cancelled promises
> They want renewed. They never learn.

That, as Peter Ferguson says, 'brings us up short, like "Or lied" at the end of "Reasons for Attendance" or "That vase" at the end of "Home is so Sad"' (*Agenda,* 14:3, p. 60). It might be argued that an almost cheatingly crisp conclusion, not for the last time in Larkin, gives the impression of redeeming an otherwise undistinguished poem.

 In general, then, Larkin chose well when he selected the poems from *XX Poems* to appear in *The Less Deceived*. Here is the conclusion of 'Wedding-Wind'; the speaker is a young woman:

> Can it be borne, this bodying-forth by wind
> Of joy my actions turn on, like a thread
> Carrying beads? Shall I be let to sleep

Now this perpetual morning shares my bed?
Can even death dry up
These new delighted lakes, conclude
Our kneeling as cattle by all-generous waters?

                                    (*The Less Deceived*, 1955, p. 15)

This is marvellously powerful and sustained; all the same, one must admit
that it is not quite convincing, the persona being just too far removed
from the poet. This problem (a minor one, which does not in any way
invalidate the poem) recurs in other poems in *The Less Deceived*: even in
the later and very well-known 'Church Going', where the speaker is
ignorantly talking about 'some brass and stuff/Up at the holy end' (*The
Less Deceived*, p. 28) in the first stanza but incongruously knows about
'parchment, plate and pyx' in the third. (Perhaps there is no reason,
though, why the habitual church visitor—he calls it 'Another church'—
should not adopt the derisive, sceptical familiarity of the first stanza; and
how many people who look at churches, Pevsner in hand, today talk only
half-allusively about 'the holy end'?)

'Church Going' has become a showpiece of the Movement. Roy Fuller
(in a lecture delivered in 1968) recalls writing 'a review of *The Less
Deceived* by Philip Larkin, a poet I was then apt to confuse with Philip
Oakes' and continues with characteristic wryness:

> It never occurred to me that this extremely well-written book, with its
> youthful charm and faint sentimentalities, would become the bible of
> the period and that one of the pieces in it, 'Church Going', would be
> quoted, analysed, and anthologised almost as though it were
> 'Gerontion' or 'Sailing to Byzantium'.

                              ('Poetry in My Time', *Essays by
                              Divers Hands*, XXV, Ed. Sheila
                              Birkenhead, 1969, p. 78)

Good though 'Church Going' is, the implications of Fuller's remark seem
to me just. As a prize exhibit of the Movement, it certainly looks right on
the page: there is an unstated orthodoxy in some circles that all
Movement poems were written in iambic pentameter, rhymed stanzas,
and a dry tone. 'Wedding-wind' provides excellent evidence to the
contrary, as does 'Going', which I quote in full:

There is an evening coming in
Across the fields, one never seen before
That lights no lamps.

Silken it seems at a distance, yet
When it is drawn up over the knees and breast
It brings no comfort.

Where has the tree gone, that locked
Earth to the sky? What is under my hands,

That I cannot feel?

What loads my hands down?

(The Less Deceived, p.21)

Many of Larkin's quite early poems, as well as some of his recent ones, take death as their subject, and in that respect this is not a particularly surprising poem. What is surprising, firstly, is the allusiveness: the early part of the poem reminds one clearly of Prufrock ('When the evening is spread against the sky/Like a patient etherised upon a table' [T. S. Eliot, *Collected Poems,* 1963, p. 13]) and the conclusion of *Doctor Faustus* ('O, I'll leap up to my God! Who pulls me down?' [Marlowe, *Doctor Faustus,* V:2:142]). The second surprise is the method, the sparseness and concreteness which seem more reminiscent of *The Review* poets in the sixties than of the Movement poets in the fifties. One of the more viable generalisations which can be made about the Movement poets is that their most famous poems tended to be sewn-up, the argument clinched by a final summarising line and rhyme; here, the poem ends with unanswerable questions, and the hands that cannot feel would not be out of place in a poem by Ian Hamilton.

'Going', like 'Wedding-Wind', employs a persona and does so with more conviction—partly, no doubt, because grief is more readily imaginable than joy. Both poems demonstrate the breadth of Larkin's emotional range; and so, in a different way, does a third short poem from *The Less Deceived,* 'Myxomatosis':

Caught in the centre of a soundless field

While hot inexplicable hours go by

What trap is this? Where were its teeth concealed?

You seem to ask.

I make a sharp reply,

Then clean my stick. I'm glad I can't explain

Just in what jaws you were to suppurate:

You may have thought things would come right again

If you could only keep quite still and wait.

(The Less Deceived, p. 31)

Presumably there are readers who find this poem trivial or sentimental. It is neither: the brusque tone carries an intensity of anger and the power of 'hot inexplicable hours' is reinforced by the deliberately bathetic simplicity of the last two lines.

One needs to have some notion of Larkin's range in poems like these three if one is to see his more widely-quoted self-deprecating pieces in a proper context. The whole point of 'Toads', if I read it correctly, with its contrast between the 'Six days a week' worker and the 'folk' who 'live on their wits' (*The Less Deceived,* p. 32), is not that the poet or his persona is entirely stifled by 'the toad *work*' but that he has *both.* And the same ambivalence is to be found in this poem's sequel, 'Toads Revisited', from

The Whitsun Weddings, where the speaker is 'one of the men/You meet of an afternoon' 'dodging the toad work' but nevertheless concludes,

> No, give me my in-tray,
> My loaf-haired secretary,
> My shall-I-keep-the-call-in-Sir:
> What else can I answer,
>
> When the lights come on at four
> At the end of another year?
> Give me your arm, old toad;
> Help me down Cemetery Road.

(The Whitsun Weddings, 1964, p. 18)

The theme of these poems is not just the boringness of an everyday working existence but the conflict of selves within the individual. To put it another way: Larkin is frequently accused of being negative in many of these poems, but the negatives almost invariably imply both the existence and the *co*-existence of a positive. And this needs to be remembered when reading Larkin's most evidently negative poem, 'I Remember, I Remember'. The poet is travelling by rail through Coventry, where he was born; he finds he is unable to recognise the place; and he is asked, as the train begins to move away,

> 'Was that,' my friend smiled, 'where you "have your roots"?'
> No, only where my childhood was unspent,
> I wanted to retort, just where I started:
>
> By now I've got the whole place clearly charted.
> Our garden, first: where I did not invent
> Blinding theologies of flowers and fruits,
> And wasn't spoken to by an old hat.
> And here we have that splendid family
>
> I never ran to when I got depressed,
> The boys all biceps and the girls all chest,
> Their comic Ford, their farm where I could be
> 'Really myself'. I'll show you, come to that,
> The bracken where I never trembling sat,
>
> Determined to go through with it; where she
> Lay back, and 'all became a burning mist'.
> And, in those offices, my doggerel
> Was not set up in blunt ten-point, nor read
> By a distinguished cousin of the mayor,
>
> Who didn't call and tell my father *There*
> *Before us, had we the gift to see ahead*—
> 'You look as if you wished the place in Hell,'
> My friend said, 'judging from your face.' 'Oh well,
> I suppose it's not the place's fault,' I said.

'Nothing, like something, happens anywhere.'

(*The Less Deceived,* pp. 38-9)

Certainly there are a lot of negatives here; but they surely imply a wry affection for the 'nothing' that happened, just as they imply a guard against bogus nostalgia. The verse—careful, level-headed, and distinguished by an overlapping rhyme-scheme—is not arid, however. Larkin, who can write moving and serious poems, here refuses to be solemn; the poem, besides ironically echoing Hood's 'I Remember', is also intended as an antidote to books like *Sons and Lovers,* as Larkin himself confirms:

I don't think that's a negative poem, I think it is a very funny poem. I can't read it without laughing, or almost laughing. . . . Really that poem started off as a satire on novels like *Sons and Lovers*—the kind of wonderful childhoods that people do seem to have. I was thinking how very peculiar it was that I myself never experienced these things, and I thought one could write a funny poem about it. So I did. It wasn't denying that other people did have these experiences, though they did tend to sound rather clichés: the first fuck, the first poem, the first this that and the other that turn up with such wearisome regularity.

(*Tracks,* 1, p. 8)

It is rather more than just a 'funny poem' and we may suspect that it was felt than Larkin allows, especially in the light of more deeply poems such as 'High Windows'. Nevertheless, a reluctance at times to take himself or his work or poetry in general very seriously is indicative of one facet of Larkin's literary personality. It should not be allowed to obscure the more serious craftsman who wrote in 1955, 'my prime responsibility is to the experience itself' (*Poets of the 1950's,* ed. D. J. Enright, 1955, p. 77).

2

Larkin's third collection of poems (excluding the privately printed *XX Poems* of 1951 and the Fantasy Press pamphlet of 1954), *The Whitsun Weddings,* did not appear until 1964. The two most obviously substantial achievements in the book are both descriptive poems, 'Here' and the title poem itself. Both poems take train journeys as their starting-points, like 'I Remember, I Remember', and this allows Larkin to use his accurate eye for detail without the poems becoming static or overcrammed with trivia (these two flaws damage the similar but firmly-rooted poem 'Show Saturday' in *High Windows*); in each case, the poet is literally 'on the move' and the perspectives shift accordingly. It is clear from the outset of 'Here' that the poem is to take in a very diverse range of landscape:

Swerving east, from rich industrial shadows
And traffic all night north; swerving through fields
Too thin and thistled to be called meadows,
And now and then a harsh-named halt, that shields

Workmen at dawn; swerving to solitude
Of skies and scarecrows, haystacks, hares and pheasants,
And the widening river's slow presence,
The piled gold clouds, the shining gull-marked mud,
Gathers to the surprise of a large town . . .
(*The Whitsun Weddings*, p. 9)

This breathless journey is by way of introduction: it is an unmistakably Larkinesque mode of writing which may equally be praised for its fidelity to experience or disparaged for its identikit generality. Now, it seems, we have arrived, and 'Here' is without doubt Hull. But 'Here' turns out to be more than one place (as indeed any 'large town' and its surrounding country must), and the tone of the poem becomes even more breathless:

Here domes and statues, spires and cranes cluster
Beside grain-scattered streets, barge-crowded water,
And residents from raw estates, brought down
The dead straight miles by stealing flat-faced trolleys,
Push through plate-glass swing doors to their desires—
Cheap suits, red kitchen-ware, sharp shoes, iced lollies,
Electric mixers, toasters, washers, driers . . .

Eric Homberger comments curiously on this: 'The catalogues are never random or pleasureful. Far from it. *Red* kitchen-ware, after all!' (*The Art of the Real*, 1977, p. 75). But I suspect that if 'red' had two syllables or if Larkin had gone window-shopping on a different day, the kitchen-ware might well have been blue. Nevertheless, the apparent randomness is deliberate and carefully sifted, and it continues with some modulation for another stanza: 'Here' is a random anywhere/nowhere, unparticularised and unnamed, though in the last stanza (and one of the good things about the poem is the way the poet's vision gradually edges towards the sea) defined in at least one geographical sense:

And out beyond its mortgaged half-built edges
Fast-shadowed wheat-fields, running high as hedges,
Isolate villages, where removed lives
Loneliness clarifies. Here silence stands
Like heat. Here leaves unnoticed thicken,
Hidden weeds flower, neglected waters quicken,
Luminously-peopled air ascends;
And past the poppies bluish neutral distance
Ends the land suddenly beyond a beach
Of shapes and shingle. Here is unfenced existence:
Facing the sun, untalkative, out of reach.

In a perverse misreading of this stanza, Donald Davie comments:

Here every nonurban thing comes along with a negating or cancelling epithet—leaves are 'unnoticed', waters are 'neglected', distance is 'neutral'. And if existence is 'unfenced', it is also 'out of reach'; if it is 'untalkative', it is by that token noncommittal, unhelpful.

(*Thomas Hardy and British Poetry*, p. 81)

I have already referred to Larkin's manner of implying positives through the use of negatives, and this is a good example. The leaves are 'unnoticed' and the waters 'neglected' by the 'cut-price crowd', which is quite plainly to the benefit of the leaves and waters; 'bluish neutral distance' is a straightforward and accurate description of seascape; the sea is literally 'unfenced' and it is 'out of reach' because the poet is at the very least on dry land, and possibly still in the town or in a train; the sea is also, unlike the crowd, 'untalkative', and this does not imply that it is unhelpful any more than a talkative crowd could be said to be necessarily helpful—on the contrary, it implies a necessary tranquillity after the breathless rush of the preceding stanzas. Homberger maintains that the 'final qualification' ('out of reach') 'is at once reassuring ... but also devastating, in that the consoling and curative resources of nature are "out of reach" of those whose need is great' (*The Art of the Real*, p.76). He does not appear to realise, as Larkin surely does, that it is precisely because the sea, like the 'deep blue air' in 'High Windows', *is* 'out of reach' that it may be 'consoling and curative' (the ponderous terminology seems ridiculously inappropriate); and that it had better stay that way. 'Here' is not a faultless poem—all Larkin's catalogues and panoramas have their cramped moments—but the careful manner in which it modulates to its conclusion is admirable.

Of 'The Whitsun Weddings' itself I had intended to say little—it is well-known and well-liked—except that it contains several memorable examples of the richness of language and cadence which Larkin can achieve. I had assumed, naively as it turns out, that this was one of the rare poems which everyone agrees about. But two recent commentaries—by David Holbrook and Richard Swigg—demonstrate that this is not the case. It will perhaps be as well to remind ourselves of what the poem is actually about before seeing what Holbrook and Swigg make of it.

The first two stanzas are introductory: the poet is 'late getting away' from Hull one Whit Saturday, when he catches a slow 'three-quarters-empty' train for London. The departure is affectionately and evocatively described:

> We ran
> Behind the backs of houses, crossed a street
> Of blinding windscreens, smelt the fish-dock; thence
> The river's level drifting breadth began,
> Where sky and Lincolnshire and water meet.

(*The Whitsun Weddings*, p. 21)

In the second stanza, generalities ('Wide farms', 'Canals with floatings of

industrial froth', 'the next town, new and nondescript') are offset by the
one particular: 'A hothouse flashed uniquely'. And then, in the third
stanza, Larkin begins to notice 'what a noise/The weddings made/Each
station that we stopped at'. The first is seen only retrospectively: he
mistakes the 'whoops and skirls' for 'porters larking with the mails'.

> Once we started, though,
> We passed them, grinning and pomaded, girls
> In parodies of fashion, heels and veils,
> All posed irresolutely, watching us go,
>
> As if out on the end of an event
>   Waving goodbye
> To something that survived it. Struck, I leant
> More promptly out next time, more curiously,
> And saw it all again in different terms:
> The fathers with broad belts under their suits
> And seamy foreheads; mothers loud and fat;
>
> An uncle shouting smut; and then the perms,
> The nylon gloves and jewellery substitutes,
> The lemons, mauves, and olive-ochres that
> Marked off the girls unreally from the rest.

As the journey continues, 'All down the line/Fresh couples climbed
aboard', and Larkin offers another perspective:

> And, as we moved, each face seemed to define
> Just what it saw departing: children frowned
> At something dull; fathers had never known
>
> Success so huge and wholly farcical;
>   The women shared
> The secret like a happy funeral;
> While girls, gripping their handbags tighter, stared
> At a religious wounding. Free at last,
> And loaded with the sum of all they saw,
> We hurried towards London . . .

Now the focus gradually alters, so that the four central stanzas about the
weddings are framed by the two introductory stanzas and the two
concluding stanzas dealing with the remainder of the journey:

> Some fifty minutes, that in time would seem
> Just long enough to settle hats and say
>   *I nearly died,*
> A dozen marriages got under way.
> They watched the landscape, sitting side by side
> —An Odeon went past, a cooling tower,
> And someone running up to bowl—and none
> Thought of the others they would never meet

Or how their lives would all contain this hour.
I thought of London spread out in the sun,
Its postal districts packed like squares of wheat:
There we were aimed. And as we raced across
   Bright knots of rail
Past standing Pullmans, walls of blackened moss
Came close, and it was nearly done, this frail
Travelling coincidence; and what it held
Stood ready to be loosed with all the power
That being changed can give. We slowed again,
And as the tightened brakes took hold, there swelled
A sense of falling, like an arrow-shower
Sent out of sight, somewhere becoming rain.

The suppleness and sureness of these concluding stanzas, the skill with
which Larkin merges the two themes of the train journey and the
weddings, the exactness with which the shape and rhythm of the journey
are caught in the poem: these seem to me among the outstanding features
here. The closing lines, in which the language remains lucid and rational
yet hints at a range of emotional connotations beyond words, anticipates
the endings of 'High Windows' and 'Money'. This conclusion is magical:
a combination of hesitancy and finality in the verse, and the recognition in
the reader that 'one knows the feeling'.

But according to David Holbrook I am wrong. He announces obscurely
that 'it is obvious at the end that Larkin feels he should be expressing a
creative moment, in creative terms', quotes most of the final stanza, and
continues:

> In discussing this poem, I find students want to find something
> seminal, something transcendent, in those closing lines. But what
> defeats them is the language. It is not good enough: it cannot take on
> the burden of the meaning that the poet wants to give the moment,
> before the train stops.

(Lost Bearings in English Poetry, 1977, pp. 164-5)

One wonders whether Holbrook's language is 'good enough'; when he
proceeds in more detail, it becomes clear that it isn't, or that he is trying
hard to miss the points which Larkin is making:

> Of course, as a train slows down to enter a metropolitan terminus,
> one feels a kind of emotion *swelling,* and this may be called a *sense of
> falling,* since the human burden that has been carried along at sixty
> miles an hour will now be turned out on its legs. But how is this like an
> 'arrow shower .. sent out of sight'? . . .Of course, the newly-weds will
> all shoot off into odd corners of London, or to air-ports, and thence to
> foreign places. But what symbolic or metaphorical act, as if from
> classical myth, is indicated? People send single arrows into the air, as a
> kind of act of chance, like flinging a dice, to find treasure or some

indication of the direction they should take. But who sends a whole shower of arrows? And what might they hope to gain from it?

(ibid., pp. 165-6)

The sequence of rhetorical questions, each further removed from the actual poem than the last, is not a helpful procedure: but what is really puzzling is Holbrook's earnest, niggling insistence on the literal. Even on the literal level, it is hard to imagine that he has never felt 'a sense of falling' as a train slows. But he has not yet finished with the 'arrow-shower':

> And why do they become <i>rain</i>? London's 'postal districts' in the previous stanza, are 'packed like squares of wheat'—but this suggests wheat ready for harvest, and this doesn't benefit from rain. The rain is, of course, in the phenomenology of <i>The Golden Bough</i>, a symbol of fertility, and so the image may be of newly-betrothed couples being shot off into the unknown, the men to unloose their seed which will fall somewhere on fertile ground, yielding offspring. But, neither an <i>arrow-shower</i> nor <i>rain</i> are fertile in themselves. A shower of arrows, as at Crecy, can be hostile. It is all left very vague.

(ibid., p. 166)

I suppose Holbrook would think them too simple, but the crucial points about this pair of images seem to be: firstly, that arrows travel upwards and rain travels downwards; secondly, that the optimistic newly-weds will indeed shoot off like arrows but that their lives will revert to something more ordinary ('becoming rain') than they have been on this special, sunny day; thirdly, that 'a sense of falling', 'an arrow-shower', and 'somewhere becoming rain' all convey feelings which one might experience as a train reaches a terminus.

I find that I jib at the inflated moralising pomposity of Holbrook's vocabulary, but his account of the poem does at least have moments of hilarity, and this is more than can be said for Richard Swigg's. Swigg is even more pompous and equally reluctant to attend to what is actually in the poem:

> But as London approaches, that approximated sense of coherence, of human solidarity, breaks up: a 'slackening ache' takes over, a braking movement which, as in 'Here', signifies that sapping of momentum 'That being changed can give'. It is not Yeatsian 'change', the perception of one movement ending and another newly beginning, but the simple process of deading that now emerges as the foremost motive:
>
>> We slowed again,
>> And as the tightened brakes took hold, there swelled
>> A sense of falling, like an arrow-shower
>> Sent out of sight, somewhere becoming rain.
>
> To make a slackening of coherence look like something religiously

beneficient, the disintegrative become energetically fecundative, is a piece of brazen suggestiveness on Larkin's part which is very characteristic.

(*PN Review*, 2, 1977, p. 12)

The assumptions, as well as the critical misjudgements, here are extraordinary. Did Larkin really intend the central part of the poem to represent 'coherence' and 'human solidarity' (which Swigg implies are good things)? Surely not: what Larkin calls a 'frail/Travelling coincidence' is just that, and I would guess that both the poet and the other travellers feel that the journey and the coincidence have gone on long enough by the end of the poem. And that monstrous sentence of Swigg's after the quotation almost defies comment. *Where* does Larkin try to 'make a slackening of coherence look like something religiously beneficient'? The emotional polarities embodied in that conclusion are to do with anticipation and trepidation, ordinarily comprehensible feelings at the end of a long journey into London, heightened by the occasion.

Neither Holbrook nor Swigg approves of the poet's attitude to the assembled company on the station platform in stanzas four and five. Holbrook accuses Larkin of sneering:

> The language has a certain coldness of detachment, in which there is an appeal to the reader to become enlisted in a particular denigratory attitude of the writer to his subject. In Larkin's poem, if we join him in this, it is not *our* mothers who are 'loud and fat', nor do *our* uncles shout smut. Other people's, the 'people's', mothers and uncles do. But there is more to it than class distance—for not only would *we* not wear nylon gloves, jewellery-substitutes or 'lemons, mauves and olive-ochres'. It is that we *know* that these are not the 'right' things. There is a kind of vulgarity, bad taste, flamboyance, and attitude to sex from which we have escaped—and to which we can feel sneeringly superior.

(*Lost Bearings in English Verse*, p. 167)

But it is Holbrook, not Larkin, who proves to be sneeringly superior. It apparently doesn't occur to Holbrook that Larkin's description might be founded on an affectionate regard for the oddity and the Englishness of it all; that Larkin, if he is detached and excluded, is in fact the lonely outsider who would like to be more closely involved with the scene; that the individual on the platform with whom he inwardly identifies (while outwardly he remains a bookish traveller disturbed in his reading) is the 'uncle shouting smut'. Holbrook can't see this because, as he insists, making italics work hard for him here as throughout his book, '*our* uncles' don't shout smut. But Larkin himself does, quite loudly, in some poems I shall come to shortly; and quite how the author of the poems collected in *The Whitsun Weddings* and *High Windows* can appear 'sneeringly superior' is a mystery (I shall come close to suggesting that he is sometimes not superior enough).

Holbrook's commentary continues for several more infuriating pages; Swigg is brief by comparison. He worries that 'the poet cannot be placed by us in any exact state of educated or class-consciousness' but feels that the poet, as he observes the wedding-parties on the platform, 'can seem (except for the stereotypes and over-tinted lighting) almost inside his moment, almost tolerantly among the world of relationships' (*PN Review*, 2, p.12). Swigg's style is again an obstacle: his parenthesis suggests that he has not grasped the intended contrast between the garishness of the people on the platforms and the intervening landscapes between stations, while the wish to place the poet 'tolerantly among the world of relationships' (how can you be among a world?) would probably prevent the poem ever being written.

Poems like 'Here' and 'The Whitsun Weddings' comfortably fit the image of Larkin as a provincial, Movementish poet, and they are among the finest poems of their kind. 'Water' does not.

If I were called in
To construct a religion
I should make use of water.

Going to church
Would entail a fording
To dry, different clothes;

My liturgy would employ
Images of sousing,
A furious devout drench,

And I should rise in the east
A glass of water
Where any-angled light
Would congregate endlessly.

(The Whitsun Weddings, p. 20)

Symbolic? Yes, but, says Colin Falck, 'there is a coyness about this poem which makes it hard to take very seriously' (*The Modern Poet*, ed. Ian Hamilton, 1968, p. 109). Falck proceeds with the caution of one sniffing out a possible enemy spy, and rightly; Davie, however, shows no such caution when he commends Larkin in this poem for recognising the 'special dignity or sanctity attached to elemental presences like water' (*Thomas Hardy and British Poetry*, p. 66). For surely the poem is double-edged: Larkin has already shown that he can write sparse, concise poems like 'Going', and this is another, neatly placed adjacent to the expansive 'The Whitsun Weddings' in that book. Its pared-down symbolism seems to operate seriously enough for three stanzas; but the fourth? In a poem about religion, the word 'raise' has a very different force in the phrase 'raise in the east' than it does in 'raise a glass'; yet Larkin combines these two ideas, deliberately and ludicrously. The poem thus unexpectedly becomes a kind of pastiche, though the uncle shouting smut would have an altogether more appropriate vernacular expression for it.

This is a favourite trick of Larkin's, the standing of a poem on its head in the last stanza. Sometimes he overdoes it: 'A Study of Reading Habits' works amiably for two stanzas as a recollection of the speaker's early reading; the reading-matter concerned is cheap and superficial stuff, so it looks as if the poem's ironic point is going to come from the juxtaposition of this subject and the librarianish title. When, at the end of the third stanza, the speaker rejects books altogether with the words 'Get stewed:/Books are a load of crap' (*The Whitsun Weddings*, p. 31), the additional twist seems heavy-handed.

No one could assume that Larkin is aiming for delicacy in 'A Study of Reading Habits' as he is in the last two poems in *The Whitsun Weddings*. 'Afternoons' is particularly interesting, short-lined but sinuous and not without touches of the Davie of *Essex Poems:*

Summer is fading:
The leaves fall in ones and twos
From trees bordering
The new recreation ground.
In the hollows of afternoons
Young mothers assemble
At swing and sandpit
Setting free their children.

(*The Whitsun Weddings*, p. 44)

This is effectively sparse, though the landscape is plainly Larkin's (Davie, one feels, would have had an *old* recreation ground—Barnsley Cricket Club, perhaps—not a new one). The second stanza brings in characteristic details of a slightly seedy middle-class world ('albums, lettered/*Our Wedding*'—cf. 'Home is So Sad'); but the poem moves to a conclusion of real eloquence:

Before them, the wind
Is ruining their courting-places

That are still courting-places
(But the lovers are all in school),
And their children, so intent on
Finding more unripe acorns,
Expect to be taken home.
Their beauty has thickened.
Something is pushing them
To the side of their own lives.

Earlier in this chapter I quoted Anthony Thwaite's remarks on the consistency of Larkin's poetic personality, and agreed with them. Thwaite goes on: 'Critics who tried to sniff out "development" when *The Whitsun Weddings* followed nine years after *The Less Deceived*, or who showed disappointment when they found none, were wasting their time or were demonstrating that Larkin was at no time their man' (*The Survival of Poetry*, p. 45). Though I think Thwaite's diagnosis is broadly correct, I doubt whether Larkin in 1946 (or 1976) could have managed or would have wanted to manage the delicate, accurate, and extremely moving understatement of the closing lines in 'Afternoons'. This quality *is* a development within the consistency identified by Thwaite.

And the last poem in *The Whitsun Weddings*, 'An Arundel Tomb', is a development too. This church-goer has obvious affinities with the earlier one; but the whimsicality of 'Church Going' has disappeared, to be replaced by a steadier and more serious though no less acute kind of perception:

> Such plainness of the pre-baroque
> Hardly involves the eye, until
> It meets his left-hand gauntlet, still
> Clasped empty in the other; and
> One sees, with a sharp tender shock,
> His hand withdrawn, holding her hand.
>
> They would not think to lie so long.
> Such faithfulness in effigy
> Was just a detail friends would see:
> A sculptor's sweet commissioned grace
> Thrown off in helping to prolong
> The Latin names around the base.

(The Whitsun Weddings, p. 45)

As in 'Here' and 'The Whitsun Weddings', one has the sense of a moving eye, gradually taking in details: uninvolved at first; then surprised; then reflective. The second stanza quoted above is neither cynical nor flippant: the 'detail' may well have been 'Thrown off', but it is the phrase 'sweet commissioned grace' which is the telling one—the sweetness and grace in no way diminished by the fact that the sculptor was (simply) doing his job. Later in the poem, Larkin's lines on the passing of time are finely and memorably achieved:

> Rigidly they
> Persisted, linked, through lengths and breadths
> Of time. Snow fell, undated. Light
> Each summer thronged the glass. A bright
> Litter of birdcalls strewed the same
> Bone-riddled ground. And up the paths
> The endless altered people came,
>
> Washing at their identity.

The jarring note of 'Bone-riddled' is deliberate, the reality of the bones set against the mythology of the monument; the phrase is also punning, since the bones provoke speculations or riddles (including, of course, the poem itself). 'Altered', too, involves an effectively pointed pun. One feels that only the stone earl and countess have been permanent and unaltered, but:

> Time has transfigured them into
> Untruth. The stone fidelity
> They hardly meant has come to be
> Their final blazon, and to prove
> Our almost-instinct almost true:
> What will survive of us is love.

This conclusion is rightly well-known, exhibiting a precise cadence combined with careful logical reflexiveness: for that famous last line is neither quite an instinct nor quite true.

3

During the 1970s, Larkin's reputation has undergone a startling transformation. His controversial anthology, *The Oxford Book of Twentieth Century English Verse,* was published in 1973 and his fourth major collection, *High Windows,* in 1974; he has been the subject of a special 192-page double issue of the magazine *Phoenix*[2]; and David Timms has published a critical book about him[3]—the first Movement poet to be so honoured. *High Windows* received a remarkable critical reception. 'It's doubtful,' wrote Alan Brownjohn, 'whether a better book than *High Windows* will come out of the 1970s' (*New Statesman,* 14 June 1974). In a long and in places very carefully argued article, Clive James identified the 'total impression' of the book as one of 'despair made beautiful. Real despair and real beauty, with not a trace of posturing in either' (*Encounter,* XLII:6, June 1974, p. 65). And John Bayley remarked on 'that paradox of transmutation which this poetry displays, on a scale as spacious and felicitous as that of its many English predecessors' (*Times Literary Supplement,* 21 June 1974).

In 1962, Larkin remarked, 'I should say my mind was now immune from anything new in poetry' (*London Magazine,* New Series, I:11, February 1962, p. 31). Some of his recent poems seem to contradict this; one has learned in any case to take Larkin's pronouncements on occasions lightly. The modulations—'developments' still seems the wrong word—which have taken place in Larkin's work involve a new density and obscurity, a modified attitude to the ageing of people and things, an alteration in the tone of his humour. The last point is in some ways the most striking and it takes us back to some slightly earlier poems.

It is generally accepted that Larkin can write funny poems. His own idea of such a poem, as we have seen, is 'I Remember, I Remember'. Other readers would probably single out 'Sunny Prestatyn', where the girl on the defaced seaside poster is described in jaunty verse and smutty avuncular terms:

> Huge tits and a fissured crotch
> Were scored well in, and the space
> Between her legs held scrawls
> That set her fairly aside
> A tuberous cock and balls. . .

(The Whitsun Weddings, p. 35)

That has always looked an ambivalent poem, in which Larkin's now explicit desire for conservation is juxtaposed with his own acts of poetic vandalism. Another evidently humorous poem, which was published before *The Whitsun Weddings* but which is not collected there or in *High Windows*, is called 'Breadfruit':

> Boys dream of native girls who bring breadfruit,
>> Whatever they are,
> As bribes to teach them how to execute
> Sixteen sexual positions on the sand;
> This makes them join (the boys) the tennis club,
> Jive at the Mecca, use deodorants, and
> On Saturdays squire ex-schoolgirls to the pub
>> By private car.
>
> Such uncorrected visions end in church
>> Or registrar:
> A mortgaged semi- with a silver birch;
> Nippers; the widowed mum; having to scheme
> With money; illness; age. So absolute
> Maturity falls, when old men sit and dream
> Of naked native girls who bring breadfruit,
>> Whatever they are.

(Critical Quarterly, III:4, Winter 1961, p. 309)

One is tempted to call this typically Larkinesque, for it certainly has some familiar ingredients: the ironic deprecation ('Whatever they are'—does the poet know any more than the boys?); the cunningly circular construction; the catalogue of details from a very recognisable life-style; the insistent rhymes. Larkin steps easily, and not for the first or the last time, into the role of a contemporary melancholy Jaques, and he creates a modified version of the Shakespearean tone precisely, especially towards the end of the poem. And yet, virtuoso performance though it is in one sense, there is quite a lot wrong with the poem: the awkwardly placed parenthesis of the fifth line is no doubt deliberate, but it is hard to see how Larkin could have avoided it all the same; in the second line of the second stanza, he means 'registry' not 'registrar' which shares the preposition 'in' and is nonsensical, but the rhyme forces the issue; and if 'mum' is widowed, then it is the old women and not the old men who should be left at the end of the poem. These flaws may account for the poem's exclusion from *The Whitsun Weddings*.

'Breadfruit' is interesting as the forerunner of more recent sardonic observations of the young; if it is in an obvious way Larkinesque, the later 'Annus Mirabilis' practically defies description:

> Sexual intercourse began
> In nineteen sixty-three
> (Which was rather late for me)—
> Between the end of the *Chatterley* ban
> And the Beatles' first LP.
>
> Up till then there'd only been
> A sort of bargaining,
> A wrangle for a ring,
> A shame that started at sixteen
> And spread to everything.
>
> Then all at once the quarrel sank:
> Everyone felt the same,
> And every life became
> A brilliant breaking of the bank,
> A quite unlosable game.
>
> So life was never better than
> In nineteen sixty-three
> (Though just too late for me)—
> Between the end of the *Chatterley* ban
> And the Beatles' first LP.
>
> (*High Windows*, 1974, p. 34)

This, says Jonathan Raban,

> might look, to the unkind eye, like the Larkin poem to end all Larkin poems ... a doggerel invasion of his own wry, well-kept poetic apartment. ... 'Annus Mirabilis' becomes a poem so promiscuous in its ironies that it turns into a maze, a stylistic labyrinth in which no directions are certain.
>
> (*The Society of the Poem*, 1971, p. 59)

These are not unreasonable remarks, but Raban goes on to say, 'The manner has taken over the reins of the verse', and to imply all sorts of stylistic significance to the poem. Raban takes it too seriously: like 'Water' or 'A Study of Reading Habits', this is a poem in which the joke is very firmly on the reader. So it is not strictly speaking a self-parody: the poet seems to have set out to write not a parody of a Larkin poem but a poem which might be mistaken for a parody of a Larkin poem. I suppose it is therefore (though the argument is getting a shade N. F. Simpsonish) a parody of a parody.

When 'Annus Mirabilis' first appeared in print, Derwent May wrote of it: 'The poem strikes a perfect balance between tenderness and irony towards the hopes of the Sexual Revolution' (*Times Literary Supplement*, 12 February 1970). Now, in the context of *High Windows*, the tenderness seems less evident and the irony more strident. There are several poems in the collection on related themes. In 'Posterity', Larkin invents his biographer, Jake Balokowsky, American of course, who cannot understand 'those old-type *natural* fouled-up guys' (*High Windows*, p. 27); in 'This Be the Verse', the bleak conclusion is 'Get out as early as you can,/And don't have any kids yourself' (*High Windows*, p. 30); and in 'High Windows', as in 'Annus Mirabilis', there is a harsher force than ironic wit at work:

> When I see a couple of kids
> And guess he's fucking her and she's
> Taking pills or wearing a diaphragm,
> I know this is paradise
>
> Everyone old has dreamed of all their lives—
> Bonds and gestures pushed to one side
> Like an outdated combine harvester,
> And everyone young going down the long slide
>
> To happiness, endlessly.

(*High Windows*, p. 17)

'Youth is power. He knows it . . .' writes Gunn of the boy in a café in one of his brother's photographs (*Positives*, 1967, p. 20). Larkin knows it too, as he indicates both here and in 'Sad Steps'. The humour has hardened, decisively and defensively: and at the same time, given the body of Larkin's work to date, one feels less and less inclined to attribute these sentiments to a hypothetical 'speaker' in the poems—Larkin's interviews, after all, tend to reveal the same kind of personality and the same kind of vocabulary. But Larkin's attitudes are seldom as uncomplicated as they at first seem in his most straightforward poems: 'High Windows' contains sympathy and approval as well as envy and disapproval. That is why the argument dissolves, as it does in 'The Whitsun Weddings', into something reaching beyond words:

> Rather than words comes the thought of high windows:
> The sun-comprehending glass,
> And beyond it, the deep blue air, that shows
> Nothing, and is nowhere, and is endless.

Only the unpractised reader of Larkin will be deceived by that 'Nothing' and 'nowhere': the empty, the spacious, the 'out of reach' are positives for him in 'High Windows' as in 'Here'. And in this poem, there *is* a religious connotation, though it is characteristically ambiguous: the high windows may catch the sun simply because they are in a tall building, or they may be tall windows as in a church (exactly the same idea may be found in John Crowe Ransom's 'Bells for John Whiteside's Daughter'). If the windows are in a church, 'sun-comprehending' has the additional resonance of 'Son-comprehending'. The conclusion embodies a feeling of release from the trivial world of 'a couple of kids' just as the conclusion of 'The Whitsun Weddings' embodies a feeling of release from the hot, claustrophobic world of the train.

Endings like those of 'The Whitsun Weddings' and 'High Windows' have to be perfectly judged if they are to succeed: the reader has to be persuaded to adjust suddenly from a primarily denotative vocabulary to a primarily connotative one. Larkin tries the same trick in 'Money', far less successfully; after three chatty stanzas, he concludes:

I listen to money singing. It's like looking down
From long french windows at a provincial town,
The slums, the canal, the churches ornate and mad
In the evening sun. It is intensely sad.

(High Windows, p. 40)

But 'money singing' isn't 'like looking down'; nor is the view from the 'long french windows' 'intensely sad'. The poem lacks the energy in argument, in vocabulary, in cadence, to compensate for the disconnection of logic.

Larkin's early poems tended to be, or at least to look, fairly straightforward; a longish poem—or rather, three not very clearly related short ones—called 'Livings' is a new departure for him in terms of denseness and obscurity. The second of the three poems is described by Clive James as 'a case of over-refinement leading to obscurity' (James, loc. cit., p. 68), and he goes on cautiously to speculate: 'My guess—and a guess is not as good as an intelligent deduction—is that the speaker is a lighthouse keeper.' (For the more perceptive or merely more rash Alan Brownjohn, the speaker is 'a thinly-disguised lighthouse keeper' Brownjohn, [loc. cit.]). The first poem is not much clearer; I quote the first stanza for one particular reason:

I deal with farmers, things like dips and feed.
Every third month I book myself in at
The —— Hotel in ——ton for three days.
The boots carries my lean old leather case
Up to a single, where I hang my hat.
One beer, and then 'the dinner', at which I read
The ——shire Times from soup to stewed pears.
Births, deaths. For sale. Police court. Motor spares.

(High Windows, p. 13)

The poem borrows the conventions of a novel (perhaps a specific novel, though I can't place the allusions); it is set in 1929. The problem is how to read it, either aloud or to oneself; what noise does one make to fill the maddening blanks (which now, as not in the original publication in the Observer, each appear to represent a specific number of letters, like a

crossword puzzle)? Recently, talking about poetry readings in general
and the National Theatre's *Larkinland* in particular, Larkin has stressed
his own preference for poems on the page, so that it is possible for the
reader to take in stanzaic and rhyme schemes, punctuation, italics. He
continues: 'This doesn't mean I'm indifferent to how a poem sounds, but
I can do that in my head. . . . And it follows that this is the way I write
poems: to be read on the page like novels, by readers who can imagine the
sound of what they're reading' (BBC radio broadcast, 28 July 1977).
Larkin hardly assists his readers to 'imagine the sound' of 'Livings'. And
what are we to make of this from a poet who was once so firmly opposed to
private mythologies and allusions?

These questions involve the recurrent problem of the poet's relation-
ship with and confidence in his audience—which is mocked in a piece like
'Annus Mirabilis', baffled in 'Livings'. Fortunately, there are among
Larkin's recent poems a number of pieces which seem to me to reaffirm
the overall direction of his poetic enterprise. The three poems I am about
to discuss all touch on the subject of old age (it is the main theme of two of
them). The first is 'Heads in the Women's Ward':

On pillow after pillow lies
The wild white hair and staring eyes;
Jaws stand open; necks are stretched

With every tendon sharply sketched;
A bearded mouth talks silently
To someone no one else can see.

Sixty years ago they smiled
At lover, husband, first-born child.

Smiles are for youth. For old age come
Death's terror and delirium.

(*New Humanist*, 1, May 1972, p. 17)

The simplicity is deceptive. The poem starts deliberately in clichés—
'wild white hair and staring eyes', for instance, though there is a curious
echo of 'Kubla Khan' here—so that we only half-notice what is being
said. The particular comes into the poem startlingly with 'A bearded
mouth' (an image which seems to haunt Larkin—see 'Faith Healing') but
is swept away again by 'they' in line 7. Then in the next line, the plural
'they' is fragmented into individual component parts—'At lover,
husband, first-born child.' Larkin has achieved a general statement
which jolts us into a realisation of the particular; and he has achieved it in
a form which is, even for him, unusually simple and traditional.

'To the Sea' consolidates Larkin's position as a master of the long
retrospective glance: the poem catches the eye and urges it, in an ir-
resistible infinitive opening, 'To step over the low wall that divides/Road
from concrete walk along the shore . . .' (*High Windows*, p. 9). We are

pushed through an almost-familiar descriptive catalogue (the piece bears a merely superficial resemblance to 'Here') until, with characteristic sleight of hand, the author nudges us to a more sombre and enigmatic conclusion:

> The white steamer has gone. Like breathed-on glass
> The sunlight has turned milky. If the worst
> Of flawless weather is our falling short,
> It may be that through habit these do best,
> Coming to water clumsily undressed
> Yearly; teaching their children by a sort
> Of clowning; helping the old, too, as they ought.

The detail, the language, the movement of the verse all seem exactly right.

'The Old Fools' is unlike either of these poems, a piece of writing of extraordinary range:

> What do they think has happened, the old fools,
> To make them like this? Do they somehow suppose
> It's more grown-up when your mouth hangs open and drools,
> And you keep on pissing yourself, and can't remember
> Who called this morning?

> > *(High Windows*, p. 19)

Larkin's readers will not be fooled by the harshness of this opening: modulation is, as we have already seen, a major aspect of his art. There is a rage here which, surprisingly, reminds one of Yeats.[4] The poem moves from its brash and unsympathetic first lines into some wry reflections on death in the second stanza:

> > It's only oblivion, true:
> We had it before, but then it was going to end,
> And was all the time merging with a unique endeavour
> To bring to bloom the million-petalled flower
> Of being here.

Is 'being here' really a 'million-petalled flower'? And whose 'being here' is meant, the poet's or the old fools'? That word 'endeavour' implies the possibility of failure as well as of success, to which Larkin adds this emphasis:

> > Next time you can't pretend
> There'll be anything else.

However, it is not until the second half of the poem that Larkin, having hinted at various possible approaches in the first two stanzas, gets into the main flow of his argument:

> Perhaps being old is having lighted rooms
> Inside your head, and people in them, acting.
> People you know, yet can't quite name; each looms
> Like a deep loss restored, from known doors turning,
> Setting down a lamp, smiling from a stair, extracting

A known book from the shelves; or sometimes only
The rooms themselves, chairs and a fire burning,
The blown bush at the window, or the sun's
Faint friendliness on the wall some lonely
Rain-ceased midsummer evening. That is where they live:
Not here and now, but where all happened once.
   This is why they give
An air of baffled absence, trying to be there
Yet being here. For the rooms grow farther, leaving
Incompetent cold, the constant wear and tear
Of taken breath, and them crouching below
Extinction's alp, the old fools, never perceiving
How near it is. This must be what keeps them quiet:
The peak that stays in view wherever we go
For them is rising ground. Can they never tell
What is dragging them back, and how it will end? Not at night?
Not when the strangers come? Never, throughout
The whole hideous inverted childhood? Well,
   We shall find out.

This is a poetry of peculiar density: the occasional odd epithet ('Incompetent cold'), the movement at odds with the metrical norm, the sprawling self-generating syntax—these features have figured in Larkin's earlier work, but not with this sort of intensity. It is essential to recognise that the relentlessness is an aspect of sympathy, not of callousness, and to notice how firmly Larkin insists at the end of the poem on his (and our) eventual identification with the old fools. In a review of *High Windows,* I described 'The Old Fools' as 'a poem which enlarges and transcends the Wordsworthian tradition of English poetry': it is one of Larkin's most ambitious poems and one which belongs with 'Church Going' and 'The Whitsun Weddings' among the landmarks by which his reputation will be mapped out.

But the map will be incomplete if it shows only the large and plainly impressive pieces; poems such as 'Going', 'Afternoons', and 'An Arundel Tomb' are among those which best demonstrate Larkin's sometimes neglected qualities of flexibility, economy, seriousness. Larkinland—the name seems likely to stick as Greeneland has to Graham Greene—has its obvious limits and dangers: chief among the dangers, it seems to me, is a tendency, in poems like 'A Study of Reading Habits', 'Sunny Prestatyn', and 'This Be the Verse', to counter one philistinism with another. Yet criticism can become impertinent or irrelevant if it insists too strenuously that the poet should have written a different kind of poetry and fails to attend properly to what he has written: and this is the weakness of Holbrook's and Swigg's comments on 'The Whitsun Weddings'. There is after all something to be said for being grateful for what is there.

NOTES

1. See Donald Davie, *Thomas Hardy and British Poetry*, 1973, p. 63 ff. For some interesting comments on Larkin's early poetry, and in particular on those poems in *XX Poems*, 1951, which are not collected elsewhere, see Peter Ferguson, 'Philip Larkin's *XX Poems:* The Missing Link', *Agenda*, 14:3, 1976, pp. 53-65.

2. *Phoenix*, 11-12, Autumn-Winter 1973-4. This collects a number of previously published essays on Larkin as well as including several specially written contributions. It also includes worksheets of Larkin's 'At Grass' and the first publication of his poem 'Money'.

3. David Timms, *Philip Larkin*, 1973. An excellent, well-documented account of Larkin's work; the overall pattern is, however, inevitably distorted by the fact that this book appeared some months before *High Windows* and includes only a brief discussion of the (then) uncollected poems. Timms' book appeared after I had written the original version of this chapter: I have resisted the temptation to revise and expand my comments on (particularly) the poems in *The Less Deceived* in the light of his account, since anyone requiring a more detailed and comprehensive commentary than I have provided will find one in his book.

4. Larkin had of course tried to shake off the influence of Yeats, as he tells us in his Introduction to the 1966 reissue of *The North Ship*, cited earlier; but he was thinking specifically of the early Yeats. The energy in the opening of 'The Old Fools' is reminiscent not so much of 'Why Should Not Old Men Be Mad?' or even 'A Prayer for Old Age' as of some of the Crazy Jane poems.

Chapter Five

A PROPER PLURAL PLACE

1

In 1970, Peter Porter replied, with seven other writers, to a brief questionnaire on the state of English poetry for the little magazine *Tracks*. Shortly afterwards, he wrote to me commenting upon, among other things, the proportion of criticism in that number of the magazine. 'But criticism,' he continued, 'always tends to establish orthodoxies and I'd be happier to see more poetry of high quality printed to keep the literary world a proper plural place.' During the nineteen-sixties—that other 'low dishonest decade'—English poetry and criticism became caught in a self-destructive conflict of orthodoxies: and, though there have more recently been signs of a slow, painful recovery, some symptoms remain.

2

The conflict is not a purely literary one, and this is perhaps the main reason why it has at times seemed so acrimonious. Critics who begin by defending or attacking one or other of the predominant literary creeds all too easily find themselves discussing the media or social change or 'counter culture', and at some point in the argument the issue becomes not an intellectual one at all but something far more emotive. In my second chapter, I referred to the discussion of syllabic metre in Roy Fuller's *Owls and Artificers:* I want now to return to that book, because of rather than in spite of my admiration and respect for its author, to suggest how fatally a misjudgement of critical tone can weaken an otherwise reasonable argument. Consider these quotations:

> But kitsch has also been successful in capturing an audience that once would not have looked beyond middlebrow or, astonishingly enough, highbrow art. Not a great deal of surprise is excited when the music critic of *The Times* finds on a gramophone record of the latest kitsch the best songs since Schubert—a statement made with no doubt deliberate and possibly humorous hyperbole but implying that

Brahms, Duparc, Debussy, Strauss, Rachmaninov and Poulenc had been weighed in the balance and found wanting. A similar phenomenon may be seen in the James Bond and Liverpool poet cults. . .

(Owls and Artificers, 1971, p. 14)

Of course, Stevens was not speaking here of his avoidance of a superficial Bohemianism (if that adjective is ever really needed to qualify that substantive).

(ibid., pp. 79-80)

Of course, it hardly needs to be said that the intellect cannot be abolished, even in Hornsey. Homo sapiens must to some degree be sapiens.

(ibid., p. 120)

One could go on quoting, but the tone is plain enough. My main objection is not to Fuller's opinions, with which I generally agree, but to his method: the way in which the phrases 'no doubt' in the first quotation and 'of course' in the second and third imply that the points really aren't worth arguing; the way in which the Beatles are slyly turned into 'the latest kitsch'; the way in which the Beatles, James Bond, and the Liverpool poets are too casually implied to be 'similar'. This is not the kind of procedure we should expect from a serious writer: the polemic looks forced, the understandings appear wilful; this is the easy rhetoric of the politician, not the critic.

It is surprising that Fuller should be guilty of these lapses since in the second chapter of *Owls and Artificers* he quotes a stanza from a poem by 'Woodbine Willie' (the Reverend G. A. Studdert Kennedy) which was one of the poems used by J. I. A. Richards as a basis for practical criticism in the twenties. He demonstrates how easily the reader can be fooled when presented with a poor poem in a respectable academic context or a sentimental one in 'an OK form', but he has apparently not seen that the reverse may also be true and that excellence may be concealed in something popular or, in his terms, 'kitsch'. He recommends careful discrimination in his second chapter, and he argues his case well, but he fails to realise that a rigid division of art into highbrow, middlebrow, and kitsch, is a complete negation of the discrimination he advocates, particularly if the kitsch—and perhaps the middlebrow too—is by definition unworthy of consideration and consequently of proper evaluation. This kind of rigid orthodoxy can only lead to a lack of discrimination which is in effect a lack of attention to the claims of the individual artist:

The music critic already mentioned has recently written: 'If the essence of Bach, Mozart and the Beatles has bitten into a person, that person today will . . . listen delightedly to The Incredible String Band and Tyrannosaurus Rex, Bob Dylan, Jacques Loussier, Simon and Garfunkle, T-Bone Walker, Julian Bream, Ewan MacColl, and Stockhausen.' Again, for journalistic purposes, the list has deliberately outrageous intent. But the coupling of the Beatles with Bach and Mozart is surely meant to give the reassurance that after all the *St Matthew Passion* and *The Marriage of Figaro* are only made up of tunes and rhythms, while the appearance of Stockhausen's among the other artistically limited names has an appropriateness the author did not presumably intend.

(ibid. pp. 14-15)

Both the music critic (William Mann) and Fuller are at fault here: Mann's peremptory 'will' is hardly credible. All the same, Mann's general point is clear enough for Fuller's misreading of it to look decidedly intentional: the Bach/Mozart/Beatles connection is plainly not to imply that great works 'are only made up of tunes and rhythms' but to suggest that the artists named have all produced music of some interest. Neither Mann nor Fuller attend adequately to the individual artist (what is the conspicuously talented Julian Bream doing in that list?), though Fuller's jibe about Stockhausen is well-aimed enough to make one want to forgive the slackness of the rest of the argument.

The lack of attentive discrimination shown by the opposing faction is frequently just as dramatic. I have in mind an essay by Adrian Henri which appeared in the Spring 1971 number of the formerly sane if unlively *Poetry Review* (62:1, 1971, pp. 63-75). Henri mentions two songs about racial intolerance: Lewis Allen's 'Strange Fruit', made famous by Billie Holliday's 1939 recording, and Neil Young's 'Southern Man', both works of social significance and arguably of artistic quality too. But he spoils what could have been a workable argument about pop lyrics and their possible excellence by bringing in some quite negligible extracts, by blatant historical nonsense (he says of Neil Young: 'Not since the heyday of Frank Sinatra singing "Only the Lonely" has there been such a good one'), and by inane platitudes: 'Gone are the days of pretty boys chanting meaningless lyrics churned out by balding men chewing the stub of a cigar.' Henri's failures of judgement are, it seems to me, less serious than Fuller's only in the sense that his argument is pitched at a lower level and less skilfully expressed. But he has some positive enthusiasm: it is the negative aspect of Fuller's polemic which is troubling. The index to *Owls and Artificers* is crammed with modish names disliked by Fuller: but there are fewer signs of the contemporary artists he might be expected to like (in poetry, Davie, Gunn, Hamilton, Hughes, Larkin, Lowell, Plath, and Roethke might stand as representative absentees).

All this may appear to be a digression: so let me emphasise that Fuller's book is subtitled *Oxford Lectures on Poetry* and Henri's article was published in the *Poetry Review*. Depending on one's point of view, either poetry has overflowed into social and political regions where it has no business, or else it has diminished to a point where it can only be viewed in a broader context than the purely literary one. The distortions which can take place in this process are well illustrated by comparing the actual record of the *Critical Quarterly* (that is, the words in its pages) with the following characterisation of its editors and their intentions by Jonathan Raban:

> Both editors have .. become notorious in Britain for their role as whippers up of a right-wing, elitist backlash against the comprehensivisation of education and student participation in the organisation of universities. During the 1960s their conservative poetics were increasingly translated into broad political terms; it has been an entirely natural movement, and has dramatised, even parodied, the larger social implications of the liberal-conservative attitude.

(Jonathan Raban, *The Society of Poem,* 1971, pp. 18-19)[1]

It may have been a tactical error to have launched the 'Black Papers' on education through the *Critical Quarterly*—though little in them, apart from some Amis/Conquest silliness, could be accurately called 'right-wing'—but it was clearly a logical step, since that journal seems to be the only literary periodical known to many schoolteachers. And it is not surprising that a campaign whose objectives include teaching children to read and write with some accuracy and sensitivity should have enlisted forceful literary support. Kingsley Amis was an early convert and it is Amis who, a little surprisingly, is praised by Donald Davie for his involvement in the educational issue:

> As a polemicist Amis has been politically active of recent years— notably, and valuably, in the struggle (doubtless foredoomed, but a fight that must be fought) to maintain a modicum of authority in one situation, that is to say, for the teacher in his schoolroom.

(Donald Davie, *Thomas Hardy and British Poetry,* 1973, p. 102)

Davie's involvement in the culture versus kitsch controversy was maintained by a review he contributed to *The Listener* of *The Oxford Book of Twentieth Century English Verse,* edited by Philip Larkin, and a subsequent correspondence lasting several weeks in that journal's pages. The correspondence at least provided evidence to suggest that the intelligentsia so heavily criticised by Davie in *Thomas Hardy and British Poetry* has some life in it: the debate was one of those in which an impartial reader might find himself delightedly changing sides each week as new arguments and invectives were produced; and the *Times Literary Supplement*'s cartoon which accompanied their review of *Thomas Hardy and British Poetry*, and which portrayed Davie and Larkin as seconds attending Hardy and Yeats respectively in a boxing-ring, had an additional wry aptness.

The issue which excited much of the debate was Larkin's inclusion of a poem by Brian Patten called 'Portrait of a Young Girl Raped at a Suburban Party' and his exclusion of David Jones, Elizabeth Daryush, I. A. Richards, Roy Fisher, John Holloway, Richard Murphy, and Elaine

Feinstein (this list is taken from Davie's review). But the argument was no doubt fuelled as much by the tone as by the content of this review, from which I quote three extracts:

> How Patten got to the point of thinking that this sort of thing was a poem is a good and appalling question. What concerns us is something else: how did the author of 'The Less Deceived' (the poem, not the collection) [*sic*] bring himself to present us with this pathetic artlessness as what we should take pride in, as representing us to posterity? Recoiling aghast from page after page of the anthology, this is the question I've had to ask myself.

> To be, as Philip Larkin is, the author of many poems generally esteemed and loved brings with it certain responsibilities. And in this anthology Larkin shirks those responsibilities quite shamefully. The poems that we have loved, that we love and cherish still, turn out to have been written by a man who thinks poetry is a private indulgence or a professional entertainer's patter or, at most, a symptom for social historians to brood over.

> This volume is a calamity, and it's very painful that it falls to me to say so. I don't question Philip Larkin's good faith. There is plenty of evidence that any talk of poetry as a calling (some have thought it a sacred one) pains him and infuriates him, as so much pompous hypocrisy.

>   (*The Listener*, 29 March 1973)

One regrets (while sympathising with) the uncharacteristic lack of control and precision here. The similarity between Davie's attitude and Fuller's in *Owls and Artificers* is striking: the ironic coincidence is that though both writers would want to condemn the Liverpool poets to 'merciful oblivion' (in Davie's phrase), both contrive to turn these poets into major issues. As Davie conceded only a few weeks later, but too late nevertheless:

> Of course, it is the unfortunate Patten who has every right to complain. Having to give an example, I picked on him, and he deserves the uncomfortable eminence no more than two dozen others.

>   (*The Listener*, 10 May 1973)[2]

Quite so: it is indicative of the way in which this sort of debate has become emotional rather than intellectual or critical that the Liverpool poets are dragged in as symbols in a cultural shorthand (the Patten poem in question, whatever one thinks of its quality, is surely a trivial and insignificant one). Asked by Anthony Thwaite in a radio interview whether he felt the Liverpool poets 'had to be in', Larkin replied, 'I did, yes. I like them' (*The Listener*, 12 April 1973).[3]

Even if one disagrees with Larkin's judgement, this seems —given the level of the poem—a more appropriate pitch for the discussion. One might note, however, that Larkin's own attitudes towards Liverpool 'pop culture' have shown signs of confusion. In 1965, he commended the 'genuine blues overlaid with the hybrid and plangent romanticism that is the Lennon-McCartney hallmark,' adding, 'Will this Original Sound Of The Sixties be the standard of the eighties? I hope so' (Philip Larkin, *All What Jazz*, 1970, p. 161). Two years later, Larkin had turned sour over the Beatles: 'I can say only that the Beatles, having made their name in the narrow emotional and harmonic world of teenage pop, are now floating away on their own cloud. I doubt whether their own fancies and imagination are strong enough to command an audience instead of collaborating with it' (*ibid.*, p. 212).

It seems clear that Fuller, Davie, and to a much lesser extent Larkin have all felt that what they understand by culture is under attack from the world of pop or kitsch (one might argue—Davie probably would—that if Larkin has been less demonstrative than the others on this issue it is only because he takes art less seriously). It would also be widely agreed that Fuller, Davie and Larkin are three of the most eminent traditional post-war English poets and that Thom Gunn is the fourth. Gunn is seven years younger than Davie and Larkin, seventeen years younger than Fuller: but it would be facile to explain away his quite different approach to this subject by inventing a 'generation gap'. The last four paragraphs of Gunn's article called 'The New Music', published in 1967, must, I think, be quoted in their entirety:

'Eleanor Rigby' is rightly one of the best-known of the Beatles' songs. It is both a portrait of two lonely people and a narrative. It proceeds by means of a series of pictures: Eleanor Rigby picking up rice, waiting at the window; Father McKenzie writing his sermon, darning his socks. Each picture is presented economically and vividly, the two people solidly realised.

Eleanor Rigby
Died in the church and was buried along with her name.
Nobody came.
Father McKenzie
Wiping the dirt from his hand as he walked from the grave.
No one was saved.

The third and sixth lines are simultaneously descriptions of fact and comment on that fact; that is, they are the most skilful kind of general-isation a poet can make. The refrains ('all the lonely people') comment more widely, implying the universality of the two individuals. The song at first reminds us of Auden's ballad 'Miss Gee', but its language is more precise, the narrative is less didactic, and there is a greater humanity in its attitude to the characters.

I would like to suggest that the lyrics to this and a few other songs of the last few years (like the Stones' 'Paint it Black', the Pink Floyd's

'Arnold Layne') are excellent poems—better, in fact, than many that get printed in books and magazines. The demands of music have structured the lyrics, making some kind of stanza form necessary. And while their strength as songs comes from the interaction between lyric and music, their strength as poems comes from the interaction between word and stanza. The stanza becomes a norm to which the variables of word and perception can relate.

Such an awareness of structure is largely missed in *The Liverpool Scene*, recently edited by Edward Lucie-Smith. Though the book is dedicated to 'the Beatles, without whom, etc.', the contributors are a good deal farther than Philip Larkin is from writing the likes of 'Eleanor Rigby'. They overlook just that ordering and power that a rhythmic norm can give to a poem, a power so great that the words may survive even when the music has been lost, as it has with many of the Border Ballads.

And it is such a tradition as that of the Border Ballad or the American Blues that the New Music has discovered, a tradition that can bring about songs like 'I would I were when Helen lies' or 'Sir Patrick Spens' or 'Goodnight Irene' or 'Empty Bed Blues', in which areas of disordered experience are brought to some kind of meaning through the orderly disciplines of the understanding.

(The Listener, 3 August 1967)

There are, it seems to me, two fundamental differences between this piece of writing and most of the others I have quoted so far in this chapter. Firstly, the confident openness of Gunn's article is in marked contrast to the defensiveness of Fuller and Davie, and this is surely to be welcomed. Secondly, Gunn starts from a position of critical attentiveness: he gives pop lyrics the same alert scrutiny which he gives, for example, the poems of Fulke Greville; the treatment of 'Eleanor Rigby', in method and even in prose-style, is entirely Wintersian. Consequently his writing has the careful perceptive (and receptive) tone which we should expect from a reputable poet and critic. And his discrimination is much sharper and more telling than Fuller's or Davie's: where they tend to be carelessly dismissive of an entire cultural area, Gunn produces a useful distinction between the structured form of 'Eleanor Rigby' and the formlessness of most of the poems in *The Liverpool Scene*. Although instinctively I find I want to resist the claims which Gunn is making for songs like 'Eleanor Rigby', his analysis is overwhelmingly persuasive. But whether or not one finds Gunn's argument wholly convincing is not the main issue: what is important is that Gunn transcends the customary rigid orthodoxies and allows his critical intelligence to range freely over his subject, instead of resorting to emotive and ultimately self-destructive rhetoric.

3

A quite different kind of critical orthodoxy, and one much more strictly concerned with poetry itself, developed around Ian Hamilton and his magazine *The Review*, which he founded in 1962 and which appeared at somewhat irregular intervals until it was replaced by *The New Review* in April 1974. 'A publication like *The Review*,' he has written, 'needs friends almost as much as it need enemies' (Ian Hamilton, ed., *The Modern Poet*, 1968, p. vii). And even the magazine's enemies would admit that no comparable publication of the period was more solidly argumentative or more consistently stimulating. In a little magazine, these are considerable virtues; and the collection of essays from *The Review* published as *The Modern Poet* demonstrates that at least some of the criticism published by Hamilton has staying-power. Pieces such as Colin Falck's careful rejection of 'Larkin's particular brand of "humanism"' (*The Modern Poet*, pp. 101-110) or Graham Martin's reservations about Roy Fuller's *Collected Poems* ('he seems to lack Graves' faith that poems are worth writing') (*ibid.*, pp. 23-31) or Martin Dodsworth's reappraisal of Thom Gunn (*The Review*, 18, 1968, pp. 46-61) shows a sensitivity which transcends the usual run of literary journalism and, more important still, a proper humility before the poem itself. Nevertheless, this humility isn't always in evidence. Gabriel Pearson's peevish attack on Yvor Winters, for instance, fails to grasp the stature of the 'enemy' under discussion (*The Modern Poet*, pp. 64-74); and Colin Falck, in an unnecessarily intricate essay on Empson, lays down a set of rules for contemporary poets:

> Because Empson has rejected Imagism, I cannot in the end like what he has done. It seems to me that the Imagist ideals (essentially there in Coleridge for that matter) of concentration, clear imagery, live rhythms, natural language and a complete openness of subject-matter are absolute requirements for poetry today. In practice Empson has denied almost all of these, along with the further need for the modern poet to be in some way present at the centre of the poem.

> (*The Modern Poet*, pp. 62-63)

Falck is a clever polemicist: he knows how to invite easy assent. *Of course* we all agree that concentration, clear imagery, and so on are good things; *of course* the poet should be 'in some way present' (can he really be otherwise? or does this mean that the modern poet is not allowed to write dramatic monologues?). In any case, these are not specifically imagist qualities (Falck vulnerably admits as much in his parenthesis and a good deal depends too on what we mean by 'natural language') and Empson has not denied 'almost all' of them. This sort of criticism involves a careful closing of doors, a feigned blindness to other possible procedures. The blindness was especially evident when *The Review* looked towards America: it tended to champion, rather oddly, much the same American poets as the *Critical Quarterly*, with Robert Lowell claiming most attention. So when Gabriel Pearson says that 'Lowell's project amounts to making good the claim that literature—with poetry as its most intense manifestation—remains a viable and trustworthy means of shaping and mastering experience' (*The Review*, 20, 1969, p. 3), this could almost stand as a policy statement for the magazine. And it sounds honourable enough, except that the 'shaping and mastering' turns out to be of a restricted kind; consequently, poets like Olson or Dorn or Creeley tended to be attacked or ignored (the spoof review by 'Lafayette Conklin', 'one of the new American poets' [*The Review*, 20, 1969, pp. 65-66], though funny in its way, indicates the somewhat adolescent level of this prejudice); and English poets with interestingly transatlantic preoccupations—Davie,   Tomlinson,   for   instance—received comparatively little critical attention.

Nevertheless, within its limits, which I have perhaps outlined a little harshly, *The Review* was invariably intelligent and enjoyable. In one number, Peter Porter suggested that 'everybody reads the magazine for its brilliant massacres disguised as reviews' and wondered 'why are the poems it prints so modest and unexciting?' (*The Review*, 22, 1970, p. 39). The problem, it seems to me, is that in dismissing the precepts of Empson and of the Movement on the one hand as sterile and over-rigid, and the precepts of Black Mountain on the other as undisciplined and trendy, *The Review* left itself relatively little territory in the middle. And this shows alarmingly in the poems it printed and the poems its regular contributors publish elsewhere.

Ian Hamilton's collection of poems, *The Visit*, appeared in 1970 and was greeted with unusual enthusiasm by some reviewers. John Fuller wrote:

> In his own poems, the critical intelligence that has served his creative editorship merely validates the habit of discretion in feeling and language that informs them. He has solved the problem which lesser poets find so difficult: that of building a poem round an organic image which has the strength to free it from contortion and melodrama even when the subject is a painful one.
>
> (*The Listener*, 4 June 1970)

The first sentence seems almost entirely rhetorical (though one might question whether 'creative' is quite the word to describe Hamilton's vigilant, uncompromising and spiky editorship). The second sentence is heavy with *The Review*'s orthodoxy. Is the problem of 'building a poem round an organic image' so difficult? And is this necessarily the best (or only) way to construct a poem? Do Hamilton's poems really work this way, free, as Fuller claims, 'from contortion and melodrama'? The following, from *The Visit*, are surely melodramatic images:

> The storm rolls through me as your mouth opens.
>
> (Ian Hamilton, *The Visit*, 1970, p. 13)
> Tight in your hand,

Your Empire Exhibition shaving mug.

(ibid., p. 20)

Above us now, the bridge
The dual carriageway,
And the cars, their solemn music
Cool, expectant, happily pursued.

(ibid., p. 27)

The *Last Waltz* floods over them
Illuminating
Fond, exhausted smiles.

(ibid., p. 30)

In an obvious sense it is unfair to isolate images like this, but it is necessary if one is arguing specifically about the strength and quality of the image. The bathos is exaggerated by the line-breaks, the eccentric punctuation (why a comma after 'carriageway' but not after 'bridge'?), and the poverty of the description. This poetry is elaborately excused by the reviewer in the *TLS*:

> ... Mr. Hamilton practises a rigorous economy in descriptive detail. Unparticularised hands take up the expression burden that most poets would assign to vivid features of the face. Less often the head, sometimes the hair, eyes, or lips emerge, quite without specific colour or shape, as if the poet could not bear to look closely.

(Times Literary Supplement, 2 July, 1970)

One possible reaction is to say quite simply that the poet's business *is* to look closely: but this won't quite do, since it is obviously possible to write poems about not looking closely. The trouble with the *TLS* review is the concealed assumption, common enough in recent criticism, that the quality and sincerity of the experience vindicate the poem, no matter how perfunctory the poem itself may be.

Hamilton's poems place their entire weight on images which lack resilience. When he succeeds, as in the closing lines of 'Home', it is because he has allowed the metre and the syntax to take over some of the burden of articulation from the image (not, as the *TLS* supposes, because of the assonance of 'I', 'eye', and 'ice'):

'That's where I live.' My father's sleepless eye
Is burning down on us. The ice
That catches in your hair melts on my tongue.

(The Visit, p. 31)

The movement of the verse is exactly right: for once, Hamilton has let the poem flow and develop instead of curtailing it (even though the whole poem is only seven lines long).

Hugo Williams was a frequent contributor to *The Review* and shares some of its literary principles. It is worth comparing his work with Hamilton's: where Hamilton's poems typically pivot upon a single image,

Williams works his images into the fabric of the poem. His poems seem to me to have a density which Hamilton's lack, even though many of them are as terse as those in *The Visit*:

The disposable hypodermic slips into my biceps.
The doctor looks at me, I think victoriously.

(Hugo Williams, *Sugar Daddy*, 1970, p. 43)

The placing of the single comma—admitting a possible ambiguity—is precise and unobtrusive. Williams has a feeling for syntactical movement as well as an observant eye and a wry sense of humour. I quote the whole of 'The Couple Upstairs', perhaps the best poem in his second collection, *Sugar Daddy*:

Shoes instead of slippers down the stairs,
She ran out with her clothes

And the front door banged and I saw her
Walking crookedly, like naked, to a car.

She was not always with him up there,
And yet they seemed inviolate, like us,
Our loves in sympathy. Her going

Thrills and frightens us. We come awake
And talk excitedly about ourselves, like guests.

(*Sugar Daddy*, p. 6)

The movement of the poem is finely charted by the word 'like': from detached observation ('like naked') through personal involvement ('like us') to a new and frightening detachment ('like guests') at the end. These three simple parentheses bring a significant and painful experience sharply into focus without any of the strain one finds in Hamilton.

Before metamorphosing into *The New Review* (which does not claim to be a poetry magazine and which seems to print rather less poetry and criticism of poetry than other general literary magazines), *The Review* widened its scope, admitting not only a slightly broader range of poetry but also articles on such subjects as pop lyrics by the ubiquitous Clive James and cartoons by Russell Davies. Its mitigated sternness may have been a symptom of the magazine's struggle for survival or a preparation for the change to a monthly journal. Certainly, one felt that the greater flexibility was desirable, not least because *The Review*'s regular contributors also write or have written on poetry for the *TLS*, *Observer*, *Listener* and *New Statesman*: consequently *The Review*'s particular view of poetry has reached a far wider audience than the magazine itself. Finally, it is worth noting that Hamilton cleverly (and justifiably) forestalled a certain type of criticism by allowing his 'enemies' space in *The Review* (in an 'Opinion' section and in a symposium on contemporary poetry), and by developing a strong line in self-parody. 'Edward Pygge', *The Review*'s satirical columnist, is also the 'author' of the following

poem which is attributed to Aeon Hamilton (it is called 'Plea'):
    Above, the Muse. She listens to my plea
    And when I touch her hand
    It darkens silently. A gentle fist
    Approaches. Soon she'll cry: 'Gerroff
    Five-liner, don't you know I need another three.'
                                    (*New Statesman*, 22 June 1973)
Nor is Hugo Williams to be spared, although this parody does not
originate quite so closely from *The Review* itself:
    Shy Boy
    Girls are behind glass,
    Like in expensive shop windows.
    The others can buy without money.
    I don't know how to ask.
                                    (*Poems by Iago Hum-Wills*, 1971)
In the final double number of *The Review*, two of its contributors
reviewed each other's books in verse ('To John Fuller' by James Fenton
and 'To James Fenton' by John Fuller in *The Review*, 29/30, 1972, pp.
90-102), a gesture of curiously appropriate cannibalism.

4

I should at this point say something about a third force, besides pop
culture and *Review*-orthodoxy, which seemed to make a takeover-bid for
English poetry during the sixties: and this is the type of writing associated
with Black Mountain College, usually exemplified by the work of Charles
Olson, Edward Dorn, and Robert Creeley, all of whom were enthusi-
astically treated by their English publishers in the late sixties. The effect
of this sudden availability of a mass of American poetry on English
writing has been odd, as Thom Gunn notes:
    During the 1960s the English discovered 20th century American
    poetry. But the whole lot at once—from Williams to Duncan and
    Snyder—has proved a bit indigestible. People seem to be imitating it
    in England, but they are not yet really using it.
                                    (*Tracks*, 8, 1970, p. 9)
What has happened is that a number of imitative English writers have
failed to see how far Olson's and Dorn's styles in particular are formed by
the geographical scope of America. This ought to be apparent from even a
superficial reading of Dorn; while Olson makes the point clearly in the
famous passage at the beginning of his study of Melville:
    I take SPACE to be the central fact to man born in America, from
    Folsom cave to now. I spell it large because it comes large here. Large,
    and without mercy.

It is geography at bottom, a hell of a wide land from the beginning,
That made the first American story (Parkman's): exploration.

Something else than a stretch of earth—seas on both sides, no
barriers to contain as restless a thing as Western man was becoming in
Columbus' day. That made Melville's story (part of it).

PLUS a harshness we still perpetuate, a sun like a tomahawk, small
earthquakes but big tornadoes and hurrikans, a river north and south
in the middle of the land running out the blood.

The fulcrum of America is the Plains, half sea half land, a high sun
as metal and obdurate as the iron horizon, and a man's job to square
the circle.

(Charles Olson, *Call Me Ishmael*, 1967, p. 15)

The influence of Olson and Dorn in England takes two distinct forms:
one, an enriching one, in the work of poets like Elaine Feinstein[4], J. H.
Prynne, and Tim Longville, who have their own distinctive and
highly intelligent styles; the other, less happy, in the work of a number of
imitators. Of the imitators, Tom Raworth at least can introduce a note of
self-mocking apology, as in the opening of his poem 'I Mean': 'all these
americans here writing about america it's time to give something back,
after all' (Tom Raworth, *The Relation Ship*, 1969, unnumbered pages).

In English critical attitudes, one finds the by now maddenly familiar
polarisation. Here is Donald Davie, enthusing about Dorn's long poem
Gunslinger:

At once comic and profound, narrative and piercingly lyrical, the form
and idiom of *Gunslinger* transcend completely the programmes of
Black Mountain, just as they transcend (dare one say?) any
programme so far promulgated or put into practice in Anglo-
American poetry of the present century.

(*The Survival of Poetry*, ed. Martin Dodsworth, 1970, p. 234)

And here by contrast is an extract from a review (ironically enough, of
Davie's *Collected Poems*) in a generally excellent English literary
magazine:

It is a shame that so much ability and wit is spent on so much ado about
Charles Olson, the American 'Projective Verse' man, who lately
inspired a quite disproportionate number of poetic boors and
publicity, in relation to his own meagre ability at verse-writing.

(Simon Curtis in *Phoenix*, 10, 1973, p. 79)

After Davie's generous praise of Dorn's poem, this is very sour stuff: the
reviewer knows as well as anyone else that 'verse-writing', with its
particular overtones, as opposed to 'poetry', does not describe Olson's
intention (nor, for that matter, Davie's). It is abundantly clear that when
Olson speaks of 'Projective Verse' he means something quite different
from what an Englishman means by 'verse', and the reviewer risks
damaging his own integrity by pretending not to understand this.

5

Indeed, the whole integrity of English criticism during the sixties and early seventies was damaged by blindnesses which look feigned, misunderstandings which appear wilful. English critics were too ready to identify an 'enemy' which they then proceeded to attack with their eyes closed: that is to say, the enemy, once identified and labelled, was frequently denied any semblance of critical attention or discrimination. Rigidly dismissive critical orthodoxies are almost invariably the result of cultural nervousness and a lack of confidence in open critical standards; and it must be admitted that the three movements I have touched on in this chapter—pop culture, *Review*-miniaturism, and Black Mountainism—are all unusually susceptible to the attentions of talentless imitators and manipulators. Perhaps, then, it is not surprising that English criticism (and English poetry, since the critics and poets are often the same people) has seemed to suffer from a lack of energy, a tendency to use up its vitality in defensive gestures. In *The Review*'s symposium on contemporary poetry, Hugo Williams commented as follows:

> Poetry in England today has a single negative ability: to resist change by modifying the conditions which threaten to reshape it. It is perhaps a faithful reflection of a day grown senile. Unaware of the structure it inhabits it nibbles like a woodworm at the techniques it sees before its nose, ensuring its own oblivion as the edifice starts to crumble.
>
> (*The Review*, 29/30, p. 55)

But Davie and Gunn, at least, have shown in their poetry that the English tradition is in fact a flexible thing which can assimilate outside influences: and as craftsmen they have earned the right to experiment. A painter friend insists: 'The craft is what you practise. Art only happens occasionally.' The small number of artists who are not primarily craftsmen (Cézanne was no draughtsman, Emily Dickinson no grammarian) are the exceptions, he argues, which prove the rule. As Michael Longley said in the same *Review* symposium: 'Well-made poems endure' (*ibid.*, p. 48). After a period in which craftsmanship has been an unfashionable commodity, it may be that a renewed and open-minded attention to the way in which a poem is made, rather than a dismissive orthodoxy which insists that there is only one way of making it, is the approach which will help to unite the critical factions.

NOTES

1. Raban's oddly hysterical tone may be partly explained by his review of a book called *The Victorian Public School* (in the *New Statesman*, 19 December 1975) in which he describes at length why he did not like his public school and, perhaps less intentionally, why it did not like him.

2. Davie continued to keep this issue alive in an ambivalent poem called 'Replying to Reviewers' (*The Listener*, 19 July 1973) which concludes: 'Don't answer your reviewers./Proud Brian Patten didn't, there's my boy.' The sardonic tone of course turns the compliment into a challenge.
3. See also Anthony Thwaite, 'The Two Poetries', *The Listener*, 5 April 1973.
4. See Charles Olson, 'Letter to Elaine Feinstein', *The New American Poetry*, ed. Donald M. Allen (New York, 1960), pp. 398–400. Originally published as 'Letter from Charles Olson Received by E. B. Feinstein, *Prospect*', in Olson, *Projective Verse* (New York, 1959).

Chapter Six

NOW AND IN ENGLAND

1

Over forty years ago two Americans and an Irishman attempted to put English poetry back into the mainstream of European culture. The effect of those generations who have succeeded to the heritage of Eliot, Pound, and Yeats has been largely to squander the awareness these three gave us of our place in world literature, and to retreat into a self-congratulatory parochialism.

(*The Modern Age*, ed. Boris Ford, 2nd edition, 1963, p. 458)

These are the opening words of Charles Tomlinson's 'Poetry Today', an essay which stands with Alvarez's attack on the 'gentility principle' as one of the most forceful and articulate counterblasts to the apparently modest ideals of *New Lines*. Both pieces, a decade and a half later, seem less urgently controversial and also less plausible than they used to: either the arguments of Tomlinson and Alvarez (which are not identical) seem to have been so much wishful thinking; or else, more optimistically, the Movement poets have transcended the rather narrow limits which their critics prescribed for them. And the vivid banners beneath which Tomlinson and Alvarez crusaded—'the mainstream of European culture' on the one hand, confessional or 'extremist' poetry on the other—have faded somewhat. In particular, Tomlinson's assumption that English poetry was ever part of a European mainstream in quite his sense is a dubious one; and the implied notion of 'The Modernists' as a unified triumvirate will not stand up to scrutiny. In the past fifteen years, perspectives have inevitably changed. Of the three poets mentioned by Tomlinson, both Eliot and Pound were alive when the essay was written: and since death imposes a finality of creation if not of reputation, one might now view their work a little differently. Of the three writers, Yeats remains a great *poet* in the sense that his prose writings are peripheral, and occasionally even damaging, to his poetic reputation; by comparison, Eliot's poetic output was sparse, Pound's enormous but variable. Eliot's and Pound's reputations consequently depend and will continue to depend on their very considerable achievements as writers of prose as well as of poetry. The writers who have exerted most influence in England in this century as poets, rather than as theorists or critics or dramatists or translators, are Yeats and Hardy; and it is a little odd to find Donald Davie announcing with an air of discovery that 'in British poetry of the last fifty years (as not in American) the most far-reaching influence, for good and ill, has been not Yeats, still less Eliot or Pound, not Lawrence, but *Hardy*' (*Thomas Hardy and British Poetry*, 1973, p. 3), when Alvarez made the same point in his introduction to *The New Poetry* ten years earlier (*The New Poetry*, ed. A. Alvarez, 1962, pp. 3-4).

It seems to me that a writer working today within the English tradition—however loosely he may conceive that tradition—is likely to have enjoyed and profited from Eliot and Pound, but to have been influenced by Hardy and Yeats—and by Auden, Roy Fuller, Gunn, Davie, Larkin (the exact list will of course vary from writer to writer). And these were the names I proposed in my first chapter as being among the more distinguished travellers on Hough's 'main highway' of English poetry, which is an altogether different matter from Tomlinson's 'mainstream of European culture'. The highway is broader than either Hough allowed or Tomlinson implied: as I have indicated, Davie and Gunn have widened it, Larkin has consolidated it. Despite a number of misleading signposts (some of which I discussed in Chapter Five), a variety of English poets have recently indicated possible directions for this highway, and they need not be mutually exclusive ones. I shall not attempt the impossible and probably unprofitable task of summarising the present state of English poetry because, taking a sensible warning from G. S. Fraser, 'one finds it hard in judging very recent poetry to see the wood from the trees' (G. S. Fraser, *The Modern Writer and His World*, 2nd edition, 1964, pp. 353-354); but some brief notes on possible lines of development may not be out of place.

2

A little earlier, I described Roy Fuller as one of the four most eminent traditional post-war English poets, a description which looks both clumsy and historically inaccurate. I needed the clumsiness to exclude various poets who are untraditional or unEnglish, though that is a poor defence, but I would almost be prepared to compound the inaccuracy by referring to Fuller not as a post-war poet but as a poet of the past fifteen years. It is true that his first collection of poems appeared in 1939 and his *Collected Poems*, covering the years 1936 to 1961, in 1962: the *Collected Poems* is a dauntingly solid book, full of poems of such skill and competence that one is liable to miss the pieces which rise above competence. But since 1962 Fuller has published four remarkable collections—*Buff* (1965), *New Poems* (1968), *Tiny Tears* (1973), and *From the Joke Shop* (1975)—which dispel any reservations one might have had about the

modesty or the ordinariness of Fuller's earlier poetry and which amount
in effect to a second poetic canon.

The fine and ambitious sonnet sequence, 'To X', which opens *Buff* is
indicative of the fusion between serious intensity and quotidian language
which characterises Fuller's best and recent work: but the advantages for
the poet of this fusion do not become fully evident until *New Poems*. Here,
Fuller achieves a wryly self-deprecating wistfulness which does not (as it
almost does in *From the Joke Shop*) topple into bathos and self-pity. The
teasingly ironic introspective autobiography is one of Fuller's character-
istic modes: thus, when he writes, in 'Chinoiserie',

How much happier I'd have been
Had I put my patrimony in low-yielders,
And been less timid and considerate,
And voted Tory, and stuck to prose.

(New Poems, 1967, p. 17)

we know well enough that he wouldn't have been happier, or at least that
the kind of happiness implied isn't worth having. Many of the poems
spring from the tensions of the creative insomniac—he has several pieces
on the subject and compares *From the Joke Shop* to Young's *Night
Thoughts*—who knows that such commonplace aspirations as sleep and
happiness are at odds with his creative aspirations. The resulting stance
and style allow Fuller to range conversationally yet thoughtfully over
areas of considerable complexity. The marvellous poem 'Orders' (in un-
rhymed syllabic elevens, reminding us that Fuller has read and recom-
mended Elizabeth Daryush) starts in his deceptively easy familiar
conversational tone:

All through the summer a visiting quartet—
Father and daughter blackbird, pigeon, squirrel.
Soft cluckings in the tree announce the blackbirds:
First it was him, daring the dangerous sill;
Later brought his Cordelia of the brood—
She pouting and shivering, rather remote.
Now in her nature like all other daughters
She drives him off the grapes and bread I scatter.

(New Poems, p. 42)

This appears to be supple though fairly lightweight verse; but by the
second stanza Fuller is quoting (and 'Not really understanding') J. B.
Bury, and the third stanza brings this:

'There is no bridge between directional time
And timeless eternity,' wrote the gloomy
German; 'between the course of history and
The existence of a divine world order.'
Though far from belief in a divinity,
One sees indeed what he meant (and perhaps there

The translator was gravelled for the right word,
   As one is oneself). . .
What is being called in question here is explicitly the adequacy of words
themselves, implicitly the barriers between the natural and intellectual
worlds.
   The meditative and the conversational enrich each other; and because of
this fusion, Fuller's reflections on being, if not old, at least no longer
young, as in 'Late Period', have unusual integrity:

After a few laps my old cat walks away
From the saucer with an irritable jerk of tail:
Five minutes later is back to try the stuff
Again. And well I know the mood myself.

How long shall I settle to these discs of Brahms'
Late keyboard pieces? Yet what else but art
Could I hope now might echo and assuage
The tenderness and sadness of keeping house?
                                          (*Tiny Tears,* 1973, p. 34)

From the Joke Shop continues this development. The presence of some
amiable barminess (in pieces about the price of Marks and Spencer's
sausages or the 'oldish fellow' met in Boots' mirrored wall) should not
obscure the fact that this sequence of sixty-three poems in 'Iambics that
keep falling in in threes' is really a sustained and successful attempt to
reconcile the business of daily life with considerable meditative intensity:
poems such as 'Variations', 'Thirty Years On', 'Essential Memory', and
'Notes on Art' embody deftly-expressed cultural commentary, while in
'The Future' Fuller once again adds unexpected resonances to an
apparently domestic scene:

It's early February. Snowdrops crowd
As close and with as coy dropped heads as some
Green-leotarded, white-capped *corps de ballet.*

Dusk; and a robin sings in actual moonlight.
Ambiguous time; my birthday time. One year,
A frozen waste; another, song and dance.

Rhubarb's sore fingers peep already after
'The mildest January since '32'—
Year of my twentieth; month, no doubt (I don't

Recall!), of bonus kisses out of doors.
What wretched verse I surely then produced
(All luckily destroyed or in a trunk).

But then I apply the epithet to that
Produced in '42, *et caetera.*
I come indoors and play my latest discs. . . .
                                          (*From the Joke Shop,* 1975, pp. 60-61)

In his recent books, Fuller has often been concerned with the problem of converting complex and detailed information into poetry. He shares this problem (though I am uncertain whether either writer would thank me for the comparison) with a poet who is superficially very different, J. H. Prynne. Prynne also quotes extensively in his poems, and in 'The Glacial Question, Unsolved' he obligingly adds a list of references including one to relevant Ordnance Survey maps. Like Fuller's 'Orders', this poem has a relatively straightforward beginning:

> In the matter of ice, the invasions
> were partial, so that the frost
> was a beautiful head
>   the sky cloudy
> and the day packed into the crystal
> as the thrust slowed and we come to
> a stand, along the coast of Norfolk.
>   (J. H. Prynne, *The White Stones*, 1969, p. 37)

But the transition to packed information comes quickly:

> Hunstanton to Wells is the clear
> *margin,* from which hills rise into
> the 'interior'; the stages broken through
> by the lobe bent south-west into the Wash
> and that sudden warmth which took
> birch trees up into Scotland. As
> the 50° isotherm retreats there is
> the secular weather laid down in pollen
> and the separable advances on Cromer (easterly)
> and on Gipping (mostly to the south).

Prynne, both here and in the even more impenetrable *Kitchen Poems*, is less concerned than Fuller with explaining and clarifying, but both poets have tried to work difficult factual information from specialised prose writing into their poems, and at times the similarities between them are striking.

Peter Porter, whose recent work encompasses an impressive technical range, has also pushed out the frontiers of traditional verse towards prose. Sometimes, as in 'At Whitechurch Canonicorum', he retains a rhyme-scheme but gently undermines the metrical norm; and he too is concerned with forcing some intractable facts into the poem:

> St. Candida is also St. Wite,
> the Latin derived from the Saxon misread,
> the death clothes she sings in as bitter
> to her as when her saintly heart stopped.
> England has only two saints' relics confirmed
> and hers are one. Three times now I've dropped
> by at Whitechurch and asked her her easiest terms

for assistance. The old iron trees tend to roar
in the wind and the cloud seems unusually low
on the fields, even in summer.

(Peter Porter, *The Last of England*, 1970, p. 34)

In Porter's poem, as in Fuller's 'Orders' and Prynne's 'The Glacial
Question, Unsolved', the facts and the descriptive writing jostle with
each other and the poem's energy derives from the collision. But whereas
in Fuller's poem one has the sense of a fine poetic intelligence confront-
ing difficult material and in Prynne's one is simply numbed by the arcane
complexity of it all, Porter's lacks both subtlety and suppleness and the
effect in the end seems not prose-like but prosaic. The lack of even a dis-
rupted or distorted music seems to me the prevalent weakness of Porter's
writing.

A younger writer who has experimented with poetry-towards-prose is
James Fenton. His poem, 'A Frog', is versified from an item in the
Proceedings of the Institute of Radio Engineers (New York). In another
poem in his collection *Terminal Moraine*, 'The Fruit-Grower in War-
Time', Fenton quotes liberally from a book called *Tree Fruit Growing*
by Raymond Bush; but whereas Fuller and Prynne use quotations to
make points, Fenton seems to include them simply to demonstrate a
dubious kind of cleverness. He is also the author of a quite impressive se-
quence of poems, 'Our Western Furniture', and one of the writers of a
series of mock-Augustan verse letters which have spilled over from the
pages of *The Review* to include, for instance:

I see ALVAREZ took
The lazy line he holds out of pure habit
On HUGHES' *Crow*. I struggled with the book
But if there was a point I didn't grab it.
I thought the whole thing one enormous *rook*.
I'm told that LARKIN prefers *Peter Rabbit*.
But it is much admired in Hull by one
Young TERRY STREET, author of *Douglas Dunn*.

(James Fenton, *Terminal Moraine*, 1972, p. 58)

The jokes are not bad in themselves, except that they go on for too long
and occupy space in periodicals which might otherwise have been filled
by poems.

3

Douglas Dunn, author of *Terry Street*, works mainly in a different area of
traditional writing. He is one of a number of provincial poets—Hull,
Belfast, Manchester seem to have been the focal points over the past
decade—whose main concern is with descriptive poetry. To call a poet
'provincial' and 'descriptive' in one sentence may seem discouraging, and

there are certainly dangers in this sort of writing which Dunn does not always avoid: many of the *Terry Street* poems are about 'ordinary' people, and the language is ordinary too, accurate but flat and without the essential enlivening intellectual impetus. Dunn was associated with *The Review* and can easily slip into that parodiable and self-parodying perfunctory style, as in 'Winter':

> Recalcitrant motorbikes;
> Dog-shit under frost; a coughing woman;
> The old men who cannot walk briskly groaning
> On the way back from their watchmen's huts.
>
> (Douglas Dunn, *Terry Street*, 1969, p. 27)

That is the complete poem: and it seems to me that this piece (unlike Gunn's *Positives* with which it invites comparison) does nothing which could not have been achieved by a good photograph. Elsewhere, however, the poet musters the energy to enter his own poem and produces more than routine description; this is another complete poem, called 'A Removal from Terry Street':

> On a squeaking cart, they push the usual stuff,
> A mattress, bed ends, cups, carpets, chairs,
> Four paperback westerns. Two whistling youths
> In surplus U.S. Army battle-jackets
> Remove their sister's goods. Her husband
> Follows, carrying on his shoulders the son
> Whose mischief we are glad to see removed,
> And pushing, of all things, a lawnmower.
> There is no grass in Terry Street. The worms
> Come up cracks in concrete yards in moonlight.
> That man, I wish him well. I wish him grass.
>
> (*Terry Street*, p. 20)

There are at least elements of tension and surprise here: the 'whistling youths' turn out to be moving 'their *sister's* goods', and the sense of community in the poem is increased; the absurd lawnmower generates the poet's carefully understated comment in the final line.

The tone and the catalogued details of 'A Removal from Terry Street' owe something to Larkin, who has so strikingly made the Hull landscape his own. This may be a disadvantage for other writers working in the area who are likely, as familiar landmarks appear in their poems, to be labelled 'Larkinesque'. The style, even of titles, is infectious: the first collection by another Hull poet, Norman Jackson, contains poems called 'So Now it's Optional' and 'Will It Be Serious' (about dying). George Kendrick, who may turn out to be a more interesting poet than Dunn or Jackson, often uses the traditional metres and rhymes of Larkin's best-known poems, but adds to them, in a poem like 'The Gardens in Queens Dock', a rough-edged power of his own:

Stuart & Esplen, Mason & Company Limited...
Aldermen too stout to know themselves long dead
Still skirt these warehouses and knock
Their pipes out by the dry and flowering dock—
A ritual for the words still to be said,
Earth to be dug, where changes fall like rain.

                              (George Kendrick, *Erosions*. 1971, p. 18)

Kendrick's skill is in making ordinary images surprising: 'too stout to know themselves long dead' works well and 'dry and flowering dock' is even better; but 'fall like rain' is too close to cliché or to Larkin's arrow-shower. Later on, the poem becomes more assured:

Hull, muddling at a confluence of rivers,
Your wall is gone, your moat is sunk. Forgive us.
Time's on our side, and ignorance; so pardon
Our error, turning water into garden.
You may as well forgive, since none can save us.

A pavement between garden, street and dock,
Monument Bridge is still so named, to mock
Wilberforce, who was long ago taken to bits
With his pedestal, by Tarran, and moved. Such flits
Are necessary for water and for rock.

The rhymes, which ought to be excruciating (and in the final stanza Kendrick gives us waters/Police Headquarters), are vindicated by the colloquial diction, the spiky, even grumpy, tone. Larkin sometimes seems to romanticise the banal even when he keeps his ironic distance; Kendrick's is a more clear-headed, clear-sighted realism.

This intimacy—grittiness, earthiness spring to mind as descriptive terms but they have the wrong overtones of unsophistication—is also to be found in some recent poetry from Ulster. Seamus Heaney has had to recover from some early over-selling of his poetic reputation: among his early poems published in *Death of a Naturalist* (1966), the notoriously over-anthologised 'Blackberry-Picking' and the other more or less 'nature poems' seem much less impressive than the marvellously precise and moving poem about the death, in a car accident, of the poet's four year old brother, 'Mid-Term Break'. Heaney is a poet who can handle intensely emotive subject-matter with forceful clarity: perhaps ironically, the most successful of his recent poems seems to be to be the untitled dedicatory piece at the beginning of *Wintering Out* (1972) which has subsequently reappeared as the fourth section of 'Whatever You Say Say Nothing':

This morning from a dewy motorway
I saw the new camp for the internees:
A bomb had left a crater of fresh clay
In the roadside, and over in the trees

Machine-gun posts defined a real stockade.
There was that white mist you get on a low ground
And it was déja-vu, some film made
Of Stalag 17, a bad dream with no sound.

Is there a life before death? That's chalked up
In Ballymurphy. Competence with pain,
Coherent miseries, a bite and sup,
We hug our little destiny again.

(Seamus Heaney, *North*, 1975, p. 60)

Perhaps it seems perverse to speak of the poet's 'affection' for his subject
here. But this poem, like Kendrick's, has an honest feeling for locality
which is very different from the distant connoisseurship of some des-
criptive writing.

Michael Longley shares a geographical location with Heaney and
explores an unusually wide poetic range. He is more self-consciously lit-
erary than Heaney, more aware of the poet as technician and perfection-
ist:

Emily Dickinson, I think of you
Wakening early each morning to write,
Dressing with care for the act of poetry.

(Michael Longley, *No Continuing City*, 1969, p. 14)

As one might expect from the author of these lines, a delicate lyricism is
one of Longley's most effective styles; the following complete poem is
called 'Gathering Mushrooms':

Exhaled at dawn with the cattle's breath
Out of the reticent illfitting earth,

Acre on acre the mushrooms grew—
Bonus and bounty socketed askew.

Across the fields, as though to confound
Our processions and those underground

Accumulations, secret marriages,
We drew together by easy stages.

(*No Continuing City*, p. 46)

One can see why Longley admires Emily Dickinson: like her, he aims
here for an absolute metrical simplicity and purity of rhyme given vitality
by unexpected words like 'socketed', though I am less happy about
'reticent' which seems to imply that the earth could, if it wished, be talka-
tive.

By an odd coincidence, the poem which has most impressed me from
this group of Ulster writers is also about mushrooms, and this is Derek
Mahon's 'A Disused Shed in County Wexford', a poem whose con-
struction—gradual focusing-in introduction, central detailed des-
criptive section, conclusion hinting at general applications—recalls

Larkin's more ambitious pieces. The opening stanza or so (which keeps
us asking: what is the point of this sentence? what is this poem *really*
going to be about?) is splendidly controlled :

Even now there are places where a thought might grow—
Peruvian mines, worked out and abandoned
To a slow clock of condensation,
An echo trapped for ever, and a flutter of
Wild flowers in the life-shaft,
Indian compounds where the wind dances
And a door hangs with diminished confidence,
Lime crevices behind rippling rain-barrels,
Dog-corners for shit-burials;
And in a disused shed in County Wexford,

Deep in the grounds of a burnt-out hotel,
Among the bath-tubs and the wash-basins
A thousand mushrooms crowd to a keyhole.

                                   (*The Snow Party*, 1975, p. 36)

The mushrooms, once we have reached them, are anthropomorphised
and become the main subject of the poem: that keyhole is 'the one star in
their firmament/Or frames a star within a star.'

They have been waiting for us in a foetor of
Vegetable sweat since civil-war days,
Since the gravel-crunching, interminable departure
Of the expropriated mycologist.
He never came back, and light since then
Is a keyhole rusting gently after rain.
Spiders have spun, flies dusted into mildew
And once a day, perhaps, they have heard something—
A trickle of masonry, a shout from the blue
Or a lorry changing gear at the end of the lane.

There are four stanzas of this sort of description, veering between the
mushrooms and the passing of time; then in the sixth and final stanza
comes the expected development into a more general argument:

They are begging us, you see, in their wordless way,
To do something, to speak on their behalf
Or at least not to close the door again.
Lost people of Treblinka and Pompeii!
Save us, save us, they seem to say;
Let the god not abandon us
Who have come so far in darkness and in pain.

Despite the risks taken here, the poem remains coherent both as literal,
meticulous description and as a sustained metaphor of oppression.

Kendrick, Heaney, Longley, and Mahon have all been published in the
Phoenix Pamphlet Poets series by Harry Chambers, editor of the maga-

zine *Phoenix* and of the *Peterloo Poets*. Others in Chambers' group of 'new or neglected poets' include three Manchester writers—John Ashbrook, Glyn Hughes, and Harold Massingham—and two notable rediscoveries, Stanley Cook and F. Pratt Green. The *Critical Quarterly*, like Chambers' various enterprises, has for some years been edited from Manchester and so, since 1973, have *Poetry Nation (PN Review)* and the publications of Carcanet Press.

4

I want to mention here two more poets who have been published by Harry Chambers in pamphlet and in hardback form, and who do not fit into the rather arbitrary structures of the preceding sections of this chapter. They do, however, illustrate important aspects of the present state of 'main highway' English poetry. The first is John Mole, whose 'Recollections of a Feudal Childhood' I quote in its entirety:

Our gardener swilled his elevenses
From a cracked cup kept for the purpose
In the kitchen cupboard. This was not
On account of his having anything contagious
My mother explained, it was simply because
He expected a cracked cup—

But I was eight. I went and asked him
Why he expected it—why was it kept
In the kitchen? Did he know about
The ones we gave our visitors, a complete set
Kept in the dining-room, with saucers
And plates of the same pattern?

And did he know (for the fit was on me)
That our teaspoons were real silver,
That our fish-knives had pearl handles
And our napkins rings of polished leather,
Did he? But I came back to the point, again
I asked about the cracked cup.

He smiled. I think he might have answered
But my mother called me in
To wash my hands and lay the table,
That was my job, she explained, the garden
His. Then, after lunch, I helped clear up;
Back on its shelf went the cracked cup.

(*The Love Horse*, 1973, p. 11)

This is probably not Mole's best poem, nor is it a 'typical' one (he more often uses a shorter line, a more clipped style). But it is a good example of

some contemporary characteristics, the least admirable of which is a pec-
uliar slackness of punctuation. It is metrical, but unobtrusively; it has a
minimum of rhyme (apart from the final couplet, lines 2 and 4 of each
stanza have fairly dubious half-rhymes); it describes a recognisably 'real'
occurrence in a deliberately plain style. One can see how it relates to the
poetry of the fifties—not so much to Davie or Gunn as to Amis or Wain:
and it is in an important way better than Amis or Wain because it is less
precious, less coy, less ingratiating. If it is a modest poem, it is not a
humble or apologetic or self-deprecating one. The diction is remarkably
natural, the string of questions in the second and third stanzas speeding
up the verse in exactly the right way; and (a small point but a telling one)
the line-break between 'garden' and 'His' in the last stanza gives precisely
the required pause and emphasis.

Yet Mole's considerable virtues of ease, fluency, and naturalness of
diction are closely related to his weakness. His two subsequent full-length
collections—*A Partial Light* (1975) and *Our Ship* (1977)—seem to con-
tain too many poems based entirely on the neat observation of everyday
scenes and events: one is at times reminded of Roy Fuller, but whereas
Fuller's poems usually modulate from trivial starting-point to thoughtful
reflection Mole's tend to remain much closer to the surface. He is in
danger of seeming to be merely a poetic joker, like Gavin Ewart or
Kingsley Amis. Having said that, one must add that some of his joke-
poems are wonderfully on-target, like this one, the first of two 'Profiles'
constructed entirely of educational jargon:

> We've found he has a concentration
> problem motivating
> major headache situation
>
> problems of relating
> to his headache situation
> situations though the problem
>
> with our problem is a
> language situation problem and our
> language is a problem situation
>
> we do not relate to
> since we never call a headache headache
> though we understand.

(Our Ship, 1977, p. 38)

Peter Scupham's first pamphlet collection, *The Small Containers* (1972),
opened with two 'Introductions': one in prose, like those in most of the
other *Phoenix* pamphlets, the other a poem entitled 'Man on the Edge'.
In the prose 'Introduction', Scupham, adopting Stephen Spender's dis-
tinction, hoped to be a 'transparent' poet like Auden rather than an
'opaque' poet like Dylan Thomas; and the poems in *The Small Containers*

are at least transparent in the sense that they announce their concerns clearly if not always quite honestly. The 'repertoire' (Scupham's own word, and a revealing one, from 'Small Pets') is ostensibly domestic: heirlooms; children drawing, playing; visits to doctor, eye clinic. But the poems invariably ritualise their subjects: an actual funeral informs the first two poems and the 'Small Pets' are accorded 'gay funeral'; a college reunion becomes a 'Wake' and a 'Lying in State'; the eye clinic is compared to Purgatory; wolves haunt the children, 'And Goat shivers, tethered in the Zodiac'. Despair is headed off, but only just, by a kind of determined play-acting in which the various resonances of 'play' and 'act' seem equally apt. In 'Arena', the last poem of *The Small Containers* (though subsequently included in *The Hinterland*), the poet contemplates puppets and asks his son:

> 'How do they work, Giles?'
> 'By magic.' Then, corrective, the quick codicil:
> 'By string.'   (*The Hinterland,* 1977, p. 45)

And though in his closing lines Scupham may cast his vote for magic, the poems too work by string. A similar tension underlies the other 'Introduction', 'Man on the Edge':

> He laughs much, with what could nearly be innocence,
> Tickling himself with feathers of nonsense;
> His words all lean sideways, blown by his eloquence.
>   (*The Small Containers,* 1972, p. 8)

The crucial word, of course, is 'nearly'.

Scupham's subsequent work can be seen as a series of attempts to exploit, rather than necessarily to resolve, the tensions between magic and string, (nearly) innocence and experience. His first full-length collection, *The Snowing Globe,* is especially interesting for its refinement of the rather crude prototypes in *The Small Containers.* The 'Man on the Edge' style, a catalogue of bits and pieces related more by magic than by logic, is jauntily indulged in 'Lessons in Survival':

> To stay good currency with your heart solvent,
> Be a pink bus ticket used as a bookmark,
> A maidenhair fern, pressed but eloquent.
>
> Look for a hidey-hole, cosy or dark,
> Where no peekaboo finger or eye can excite
> A meddlesome bigwig to poke and remark.
>   (*The Snowing Globe,* 1972, p. 37)

Such nearly innocent 'feathers of nonsense' as these are more serious (and more defensive) than the coyly playful language will admit, as one realises in 'Address Unknown' where a similar technique becomes moving rather than absurd:

> House, I have stuffed you with such lovely nonsense:

All these sweet things: Clare's Poems, Roman glassware,
A peacock's feather, a handful of weird children,
A second-hand cat with one pad missing, missing.
                                    (*The Snowing Globe*, p. 47)
These lines suggest a characteristic strength of the best poems in *The
Snowing Globe*: the ability to invest domestic subjects with an elegiac
dignity while avoiding the twin pitfalls of pretentious ritualisation and
ludicrous bathos. Often, it is sheer resonant simplicity which impresses:
Alone, on different sorts of roads, we go,
Through sheets of flowers and through sheets of snow.
                                    (*The Snowing Globe*, p. 11)
The gain in confident precision is most evident in the exact, surprising
images in domestic poems: a frog 'Falls through water like a chipped
pebble'; hours 'Detonate. . . .like mad bird scarers'; and 'The rambling
bee, obtuse and hairy,/Unzips with his dull purr/The studious air' (*The
Snowing Globe*, p.18). Lucid syntax and delighted descriptive imagery
combine to give these poems a transparent richness.
  The love poems are less successful: the packed, excited manner works
well with animals and objects, less well with people. Plainly, Scupham
has been worried by this: in some early poems he moves towards a self-
conscious compensatory brashness; a little later, in the group of love
poems collected as *The Gift* (1973), he teeters on the brink of self-parody.
The Gift needs its subtitle, 'Love Poems', for a reader might otherwise
view the poems merely as manifestations of a somewhat mannered,
precious connoisseurship. And this, so far, is the major problem with
Scupham's poetry: the implicit rejection of a Wordsworthian quotidian
norm tends to bring with it hints of apparent insincerity, ventriloquism.
  Prehistories (1975) and *The Hinterland* (1977) indicate ways of over-
coming this problem. In *Prehistories* the finest effects come, as before,
from the juxtaposition of familiar detail and startling image, but the scope
is widened both geographically and historically:
Beyond the dented churns, the huddled farmyard,
Look, a green and lackadaisical finger
Reveals a hair-line fracture in the land.
                                    (*Prehistories*, 1975, p. 4)
Here, in the opening stanza of 'Public Footpath to', the signpost as 'a
green and lackadaisical finger' leads us firmly into both poem and land-
scape (though do either fingers or signposts *reveal* anything?) with the
right combination of lightness and descriptive accuracy. The same kind
of motif reappears later on ('a church tower makes her slight invitation'),
and throughout the poem one has the sense of the landscape doing the
work, taking the initiative, until overpowered by the concluding image of
'one self-sufficient tractor/Dragging the sullen landscape down to
earth'—an image equally effective in its literal truthfulness and in its

confident note of resolution.

The greater geographical openness is accompanied by a firmer historical awareness and the two merge in the geological themes which recur through the book, though most explicitly in 'Excavations' and the title sequence: 'deepening' seems the right word for the development, in more than one sense. The sequence which concludes *Prehistories* and gives the book its title has been noticed chiefly for the line 'Ghosts are a poet's working capital' which is, in fact, too facile a formula to describe Scupham's enterprise and typical of the poet's tendency to form striking epigrammatic lines from half-truths (his 'nearly' innocence at work again). The most interesting thing about the sequence seems to me rather the first poem which begins:

Adrowse, my pen trailed on, and a voice spoke:
'Now, you must read us "Belknap".' My book was open.

I saw their faces; there were three of them,
Each with a certain brightness in her eyes.

I would read 'Belknap'. Then a gardener's shears
Snipped fatefully my running thread of discourse.

And in my indices, no poem upon which
I could confer this honorary title.

(Prehistories, p. 54)

As a reflexive (self-generating and self-analysing) poem, this is a long way from 'Man on the Edge'; it is also a poem which does not need to pretend that it works by magic and not by string. It is at once honest and magical.

'If poetry is concerned with knowledge', Scupham wrote in that first 'Introduction', 'Auden is surely right when he calls it a game as well' (*The Small Containers*, p. 6). He has been a formalist, a game-player as well as a role-player, from the start: he has consistently adopted regular metrical forms and often strict rhyme schemes such as *terza rima*, so that much of his work has the structure but not the texture of the Movement. This formal interest is explored in the 'Hungarian' sonnet sequence which gives its title to *The Hinterland*—a sequence whose enmeshed themes include two world wars, the hot summer of 1975, and Dutch elm disease. Elsewhere in this third full-length collection, there are signs that Scupham's diction is becoming less clogged and clotted than it has sometimes seemed. 'Minsden', for example, despite the echoes of Larkin's 'An Arundel Tomb' which the theme and metre inevitably produce, is admirably direct and uncluttered:

Ground shakes to sun: the rough infill
Glimmers about the nave and chancel

Where history, historian lie.
Recorder and recorded dead;

His granite flake split, slewed across,
Dark table for a sunburnt head
Of votive flowers: the twist and tie
Of camomile, corn, scabious.
Black flint secretes a fuller shade:
Cool gold strikes out across the glade.

(*The Hinterland,* p. 9)

Nevertheless, the choiceness of Scupham's vocabulary continues to impose limitations which may not always be beneficial or intentional. In 'As the Rain Falls', a beautifully observed poem, the language creates a detachment too jarringly at odds with the intimacy of the subject:

They go about some job, as the rain falls,
Or to allotments at the town's coarse fringes,
Pausing for corner-talk in words rubbed dry
By the abrading seasons. Back home,
Dull boots unlaced, they cark at meddling children.

(*The Hinterland,* p. 49)

The dismissiveness of 'corner-talk' and the archaism of 'cark' undermine, perhaps deliberately, one's sense of the poet's sympathy with his subject. And although this may be deliberate, the most worrying limitation of Scupham's mandarin style must be that there are vast areas of life and language which could not, one feels, get into his poems, even if he wanted them to.

5

Here for a few short years
Strengthen affections; meet,
Later, the dull arrears
Of age, and be discreet.

The angry blood burns low.
Some friend of lesser mind
Discerns you not; but so
Your solitude's defined.

Write little; do it well.
Your knowledge will be such,
At last, as to dispel
What moves you overmuch.

(Yvor Winters, *Collected Poems* 1963, p. 73)

Winters' poem 'To a Young Writer', written in 1930, still contains good advice—and reassurance—for the undergraduate poet. Three poets who seem to have taken the advice, and some of the style, of Winters are Dick Davis, Clive Wilmer, and Robert Wells, all of whom read English at King's College, Cambridge, in the late sixties and whose work appeared in *Shade Mariners* in 1970. Wilmer is justifiably anxious to dismiss the idea of a 'Wintersian conspiracy' and to point out that these writers were not 'exact contemporaries' at Cambridge (Letter in *PN Review*, 4, 1977, pp. 54-55). It is clear that the influence of Winters originally reached Davis, Wilmer, and Wells (and other poets) through the agency of an intervening generation; and Tony Tanner, in his Introduction to *Shade Mariners*, names the mediator though not the mediator's mentor:

> These three poets know each other and inevitably they share some preoccupations and interests. Nevertheless one can recognise a quite distinctive tone of voice in the work of each of them. They would all acknowledge the influence of some contemporary poets—notably Thom Gunn; individually they have been influenced by such different writers as Emily Dickinson, Tennyson, and William Collins respectively.
>
> (*Shade Mariners*, ed. Gregory Spiro, 1970, p. 7)

It would be foolish as well as impertinent to discuss in detail the work of these three poets at this stage: Dick Davis's first full-length collection, *In the Distance*, appeared in 1975; Robert Wells', *The Winter's Task*, in 1977; and Clive Wilmer's, *The Dwelling-Place*, is not published at the time of writing, though scheduled for late 1977. But one may point briefly in each to virtues of clarity and control allied to a confidence in language and a welcome degree of seriousness about the business of making poems. Davis's dedicatory quatrain in memory of his brother, though a little too reminiscent of George Barker's 'To My Mother', plainly demonstrates these characteristics:

> Distant, most dear; dearer, more distant than
> Ever in life, this music that I hear
> Can never reach to you, nor these words span
> The waste to you, whom I still love and fear.
>
> (*In the Distance*, 1975, p. 5)

Davis and Wells (and to a much lesser extent Wilmer) resemble Gunn in their ability to make curiously rich and sensuous poems from plain language and strict metres. Consider the extreme delicacy within rigour of Davis's 'Childhood' (dedicated to Wells):

> Imperceptible, at sunrise, the slight
> Breeze stirs the dreaming boy, till silently
> He edges free from sleep and takes the kite,
> Huge on his shoulders like an angel's wings,
> To climb the hill beyond the drowsing city.
> Released, the first ungainly waverings
> Are guided out, above the still valley,
> Constrained to one smooth flow, diminishing
> Until the pacing boy can hardly see
> The dark dot shift against the constant blue:

He squats and stares: in his hand the taut string
Tugs, strains—as if there were still more to do.

(In the Distance, p. 26)

That questing urgency is very like Gunn: and, with the inevitability of a
perfect cadence, one finds that Gunn has commented with enthusiasm on
this very poem in a review of *In the Distance* (*Thames Poetry*, 2, 1976,
pp. 59-62) which is so intimately meditative in tone that it is almost as if
Gunn is reflecting on his own poems.

It is the Gunn of *Moly* (poems like 'The Fair in the Woods' and
'Sunlight') who is most often recalled in *The Winter's Task*; but to des-
cribe Wells therefore as 'the Thom Gunn of a rural scene', as John Mole
does (*Times Literary Supplement*, 12 August 1977) is wide of the
mark. The urban epigrammatic poems towards the end of Wells' book be-
come as haunting with re-reading as the sometimes more substantial rural
pieces near the beginning. I quote, from the middle of the book, a poem
which is both rural and marvellously concise, called 'After Haymaking':

The last bale placed, he stretched out in the hay.
   Its warmth and his were one.
He watched the fields beneath the weakening day
And felt his skin still burning with the sun.

When it was dusk, he moved. Between his skin
   And clothes the sweat ran cold.
He trembled as he felt the air begin
To touch and touch for what it could not hold.

(The Winter's Task, 1977, p. 39)

Intelligence and truth to physical experience are perfectly matched here.

On the strength of Clive Wilmer's poems in three anthologies, *Shade
Mariners, Poetry Introduction 2* (1972), and *Ten English Poets* (1976), it
seems likely that *The Dwelling-Place* will prove to be as interesting if less
tightly structured than Davis's and Wells' collections. But in the first
paragraph of my first chapter I quoted a remark of Graham Hough's
which I must return to now: 'Crystal-gazing as a critical method had
better be reduced to a minimum' (*Image and Experience*, p. 56).

6

If I had been attempting to write a history or a comprehensive survey of
contemporary English poetry, I would have included chapters on Ted
Hughes and Charles Tomlinson and lengthy sections on such writers as
John Fuller and Anthony Thwaite; I would have dealt at some length
with a number of older and influential poets; I would have described the
influence on English verse of some traditional American poets (Robert
Frost, W.D. Snodgrass, Anthony Hecht, in particular); and I would have
considered the work of some writers who have not published collections

but who have appeared in little magazines and pamphlets from small presses. But my survey would have been either partial and inaccurate or else a mere catalogue of names. Even within my deliberately limited scope, new books, new poems, new essays have often made what I wrote a month or a week earlier look out of date.

In the preceding pages I have been concerned with poems—usually individual poems—rather than with trends and generalisations. But trends, of a sort, emerge. Probably England has, as Donald Davie has suggested more than once, more serious and scrupulous poets than it deserves: it is not a bad time for poetry, for it is possible to buy, with bankrupting frequency, new collections of poetry which give real pleasure in their intelligence and craftsmanship. It is not a bad time for poetry but it is a bad time for readers. We have not yet recovered fully from that low dishonest decade, the sixties, which splintered and shattered cultural criteria, turning serious writers into madmen and frivolous writers into pop stars. It used to be true to say that poetry is written and read in the universities: Graham Hough said just this in a passage cited in my first chapter, and no doubt it is still true of the luckier universities. But a couple of years ago I had the disheartening experience of visiting for the first time a university, previously known to me only by the good reputation of some of its English faculty, to read, with Peter Scupham, to an audience presumably interested in poetry. In the discussion which followed the reading, no one in the audience (except the former pupil of mine who had invited us) showed the slightest interest in the craft of poetry, in the work of the poets discussed in this book, or in the journals which publish intelligible poetry and criticism. Instead, it was evident that the so-called 'Liverpool poets' and their followers continued to command not just a popular audience of bored and disaffected adolescents but a supposedly educated audience of individuals who had chosen (and *been* chosen) to spend three or more years studying the great works of English Literature.

So who *reads* poetry now? It is a question which invites facile answers, and the best one can do is to evade it. Almost anyone: anyone, that is, who is lucky enough to live near a bookshop or a library which knows that poems exist, and who has discovered the fatuity and futility of most pop media, pop poetics, pop politics, pop music. But whereas a generation ago such people would be found in the universities, I fear that they are now as rare in some universities as they are anywhere else. This is both good and bad. It is good because it holds out the hope of a broadly-based intelligentsia which is something other than exclusively middle-brow and middle-class or exclusively academic. It is bad because it erodes the identifiable centres to which those who seek good books and good company can turn (the decline of some university booksellers is a sad index of this change). And it is neither good nor bad but incontrovertibly

difficult because it makes the business of communication between writer
and audience more complicated: the editor or publisher who knows he
can rely upon an educated audience in the major universities has his
distribution problem eased and his writers know who, in the main, they
are likely to be addressing. But who now reads *Critical Quarterly* and
Encounter and *London Magazine* and *PN Review*? And who buys the new
books of poetry put out by such brave publishers as Carcanet, Faber,
Oxford, Secker and Warburg? I don't know, beyond venturing the guess
that the proportion of undergraduate readers and buyers has shrunk
dramatically.

   Whoever and wherever they are, the audience remains pitiably small.
England is still a country where most moderately intelligent people will
complain about the banality of the daily newspaper or the television but
where hardly any of them will read an intelligent journal or book instead.
Yet, looking back over the past thirty years, one of the most consistent
features of literary life has been the urgent feeling that this audience of
'common readers' must be reached or, indeed, brought into being. The
urgency is strikingly evident in Donald Davie's 'Editorial' in *PN Review*
2:

> What cannot be forgiven us is that we appear to think there is a British
> public—that is to say, a section of the British electorate—for whom the
> furthest reach of mental exertion about national affairs is not watch-
> ing drooping-eyed Harold Macmillan interviewed by Robin Day, or
> runny-eyed Harold Wilson talking to David Frost. The actual or
> potential existence of such a public is what neither booksellers nor
> party managers can dare to admit. . . .
>
>   (*PN Review*, 2, 1977, p. 1)

And in C. H. Sisson's 'Editorial' in *PN Review* 3:

> Our concern is the less popular one of giving circulation to good writ-
> ing, and the discussion of ideas which get less than their share of exer-
> cise in other fora. Our problem is therefore with an audience which is
> not yet there or—less ambitiously—with one which is just beginning
> to appear, here and there, in a scattered way, but is not large enough to
> command the addresses of the most widely known newspapers and
> periodicals.
>
>   (*PN Review*, 3, 1977, p. 1)

The tone of these editorials is unusually and admirably resolute, but the
underlying hope is not new. Imagine 'a useful and informative journal
which will serve the needs of all intelligent readers', whose editors feel
that 'If one day a good poet can expect to sell some thousands of copies of
his new volume, then we should feel we were achieving what we set out to
accomplish'. The editors of the journal also claim that the existence of the
organisation which publishes it 'is a sign that dons today are looking out-
side their university walls, and feeling a need to offer what they under-

stand of traditional culture to the general educated public. It is equally a sign that the common sense of the reading public is recalling criticism from what it threatened to become—a sterile specialism for university teachers only.' Thus the editors of *The Critical Survey* (I:1, 1962, pp. 4-5) launched their publication into a decade in which large sections of that 'general educated public' seemed decisively to lose that prized 'common sense'.

The sustaining belief is in the *centrality* of poetry—which does not imply mediocrity nor middlebrowism nor necessarily a political 'centrality'. Donald Davie again:

> ... there is *no* analogy between artistic forms and social and political forms. ... No English poet of the past was more radical, in every sense, than Walter Savage Landor; and no English poet had an idea of form more rigorously classical. Thus, *certainly* we have to resist the impudent attempt of the revolutionary Left to lay a privileged claim to our poetry. And yet... what other body of political opinion has valued poetry enough to make such a take-over bid? If, as I think, *Poetry Nation* represents another bid, this time from the Centre—well, heaven knows, it was high time! And I support the venture with all my heart.
>
> (*Poetry Nation*, 1, 1973, pp. 57-58)

That is plainly the voice of the poet-scholar in the seventies. But so, surely, is this:

> And if the diction of much contemporary poetry is either moodily imprecise, slack, or inflated, that, no doubt, has something to do with the difficulty of taking a stand. In the last ten years, we have all had too much to digest. ... .and our natural mood, in consequence, of mild, sad resignation is not one that makes for very inspiriting poetry. We find personal compensations for the general state of stale, continuing crisis, but it is hard to give these a general poetic relevance. The remedy for our present slugged condition is certainly not to go back to the 1930s, to shout dead slogans, and fight old battles again: (like, for instance, Mr. Roy Fuller, hammering away at his pet word, '*bourgeois*', at a time when most sane people are probably profoundly grateful for the liberal, the rational, the sensitive and the humane elements in the middle-class tradition).

This is a trick, of course, and the tone of the reference to Roy Fuller gives it away. Late seventies? Late sixties? Late fifties? In fact, the passage is from the late forties: it is G. S. Fraser in 'Some Notes on Poetic Diction' (*Penguin New Writing*, 37, 1949, pp. 127-8). But how familiar phrases like 'mild, sad resignation' and 'the general state of stale, continuing crisis' seem in the late seventies; and how widely the second part of Fraser's parenthesis would be accepted today.

These general reflections, however, go against the grain and defy the resolutions of the pages that preceded them: 'what must be attended to is the behaviour of literature itself,' wrote Hough (*Image and Experience*, p. 4), and with the exception of this codicil I have tried to follow his advice. In writing and rewriting these chapters, I inevitably wondered and occasionally doubted whether the notion of a continuing and flexible English poetic tradition such as I had in mind would stand up to scrutiny. I think it does, perhaps more creditably than I at first imagined. The 'main highway' is wide and widening, and though one would be reluctant to identify any indisputably 'great' poets travelling on it, there are at least a considerable number of very good ones (more, needless to say, than I have mentioned). And if this makes the field of contemporary English poetry a potentially confusing one for critics, it makes it a healthily open one for poets:

> After all, it's rather a privilege
>   amid the affluent traffic
> to serve this unpopular art which cannot be turned into
>   background noise for study
> or hung as a status trophy by rising executives,
>   cannot be 'done' like Venice
> or abridged like Tolstoy, but stubbornly still insists upon
>   being read or ignored. . . .

(W. H. Auden, *Collected Poems*, 1976, p. 522)

Select Bibliography

This bibliography lists: works mentioned or discussed in the text; various collections of poems not specifically mentioned but relevant to my main concerns; and a small number of related critical books and articles. The entry under a particular author is not necessarily intended to list that author's entire published work. Standard authors whose work has appeared in a variety of editions are not included. A useful highly selective bibliography will be found in *The Survival of Poetry*, edited by Martin Dodsworth; while there is an extensive but not entirely accurate bibliography (by Barbara Atkinson) in *British Poetry Since 1960*, edited by Michael Schmidt and Grevel Lindop.

Allen, Donald M.
  (ed.) *The New American Poetry* (New York: Grove Press, 1960)

Allott, Kenneth
  Collected Poems (London: Secker and Warburg, 1975). (ed.) *The Penguin Book of Contemporary Verse* (Harmondsworth: Penguin, 1950; 2nd edition, 1962)

Alvarez, A.
  (ed.) *The New Poetry* (Harmondsworth: Penguin, 1962; 2nd edition, 1966)

Anonymous
  Review of *The Visit* by Ian Hamilton, *Times Literary Supplement*, 2 July 1970

Auden, W. H.
  Collected Shorter Poems 1930-1944 (London: Faber, 1950). *Collected Shorter Poems 1927-1957* (London: Faber, 1966). *Collected Longer Poems* (London: Faber, 1968). *Collected Poems* (London: Faber, 1976)

Bayley, John
  'Too Good for this World', *Times Literary Supplement*, 21 June 1974

Bergonzi, Bernard
  'The Poetry of Donald Davie', *Critical Quarterly*, IV:4, Winter 1962. 'Critical Situations: From the Fifties to the Seventies', *Critical Quarterly*, XV:1, Spring 1973. 'Syntax Now', *Critical Quarterly*, XIX: 2, Summer 1977

Bold, Alan

Thom Gunn and Ted Hughes (Edinburgh: Oliver and Boyd, 1976)

Brownjohn, Alan
The Lions' Mouths (London: Macmillan, 1967). *Sandgrains on a Tray* (London: Macmillan, 1969). *Warrior's Career* (London: Macmillan, 1972). *A Song of Good Life* (London: Secker and Warburg, 1975). 'The Deep Blue Air', *New Statesman,* 14 June 1974

Chambers, Harry
(ed.) 'Philip Larkin Issue', *Phoenix,* 11/12, Autumn-Winter 1973-4

'Conklin, Lafayette'
'Up Your Ridgeway', *The Review,* 20, 1969

Conquest, Robert
(ed.) *New Lines* (London: Macmillan, 1956). (ed.) *New Lines 2* (London: Macmillan, 1963)

Cook, Stanley
Form Photograph (Manchester: Phoenix, 1971). *Signs of Life* (Manchester: Morten, 1972). *Staff Photograph* (Stockport: Phoenix, 1976)

Cox, C. B.
(and A. E. Dyson) 'Editorial', *Critical Survey,* I:1, 1962. (and A. R. Jones) 'After the Tranquilized Fifties', *Critical Quarterly,* VI:2, Summer 1964

Creeley, Robert
Poems 1950-1965 (London: Calder and Boyars, 1966)

Cunningham, J. V.
The Exclusions of a Rhyme (Denver: Alan Swallow, 1960). *To What Strangers, What Welcome* (Denver: Alan Swallow, 1964). *Collected Poems and Epigrams* (London: Faber, 1971)

Curtis, Simon
Review of *Collected Poems* by Donald Davie, *Phoenix,* 10, 1973

Daryush, Elizabeth
Collected Poems (Manchester: Carcanet, 1976)

Davie, Donald
Purity of Diction in English Verse (London: Chatto and Windus, 1952; London: Routledge and Kegan Paul, 1967). *Articulate Energy* (London: Routledge and Kegan Paul, 1955). *Brides of Reason* (Swinford: Fantasy Press, 1955). *A Winter Talent* (London: Routledge and Kegan Paul, 1957). (ed.) *The Late Augustans* (London: Heinemann, 1958). *The Forests of Lithuania* (Hessle: Marvell Press, 1959). *A Sequence for Francis Parkman* (Hessle: Marvell Press, 1961). *New and Selected Poems* (Middletown, Connecticut: Wesleyan University Press, 1961). *Events and Wisdoms* (London: Routledge and

Kegan Paul, 1964). *Ezra Pound: Poet as Sculptor* (London: Routledge and Kegan Paul, 1965). *Essex Poems* (London: Routledge and Kegan Paul, 1969). *Six Epistles to Eva Hesse* (London: London Magazine Editions, 1970). *Collected Poems 1950-1970* (London: Routledge and Kegan Paul, 1972). *Thomas Hardy and British Poetry* (London: Routledge and Kegan Paul, 1973). (ed.) *Augustan Lyric* (London: Heinemann, 1974). *The Shires* (London: Routledge and Kegan Paul, 1974). *Pound* (London: Collins, 1976). *In the Stopping Train and Other Poems* (Manchester: Carcanet, 1977). *The Poet in the Imaginary Museum* (Manchester: Carcanet, 1977). 'The Poet-Scholar', *Essays in Criticism*, V:1, 1955. Letter to *Delta*, 9, 1956. 'Remembering the Movement', *Prospect*, Summer 1959. 'Two Analogies for Poetry', *The Listener*, 5 April 1962. Review of *Collected Poems* by T. S. Eliot, *New Statesman*, 11 October 1963. 'Views', *The Listener*, 21 March, 11 April, 4 July 1968. 'The Failure of a Dialogue', *The Listener*, 27 August 1970. 'The Rhetoric of Emotion', *Times Literary Supplement*, 29 September 1972. 'A Comment', *Poetry Nation*, 1, 1973. 'Morning', *Poetry Nation*, 1, 1973. 'Robinson Jeffers at Point Sur', *The Listener*, 1 March 1973. 'Larkin's Choice', *The Listener*, 29 March 1973. 'Views', *The Listener*, 10 May 1973. 'Berryman', *Times Literary Supplement*, 29 June 1973. 'Replying to Reviewers', *The Listener*, 19 July 1973. 'An End to Good Humour', *The Listener*, 18 October 1973. 'The Varsity Match', *Poetry Nation*, 2, 1974. 'Editorial', *PN Review*, 2, 1977

Davis, Dick
(and others) *Poetry Introduction 2* (London: Faber, 1972). *In the Distance* (London: Anvil Press, 1975)

Day, David
Brass Rubbings (Cheadle: Carcanet, 1975)

Dodsworth, Martin
(ed.) *The Survival of Poetry* (London: Faber, 1970). 'Negatives and Positives: The Poetry of Thom Gunn', *The Review*, 18, 1968

Dorn, Edward
The North Atlantic Turbine (London: Fulcrum Press, 1967). *Geography* (London: Fulcrum Press, 1968). *Gunslinger 1 & 2* (London: Fulcrum Press, 1970)

Downie, Freda
A Stranger Here (London: Secker and Warburg, 1977)

Dunn, Douglas
Terry Street (London: Faber, 1969). *The Happier Life* (London: Faber, 1972). *Love or Nothing* (London: Faber, 1974)

Dyson, A. E.
Review of *My Sad Captains* by Thom Gunn, *Critical Quarterly*, III:4, Winter 1961

Edwards, Michael
'Donald Davie and British Poetry', *Poetry Nation*, 3, 1974
Eliot, T. S.
Collected Poems 1909-1962 (London: Faber, 1963)
Empson, William
Seven Types of Ambiguity (London: Chatto and Windus, 1930; 3rd edition, Harmondsworth: Penguin, 1961). *Collected Poems* (London: Chatto and Windus, 1955)
Enright, D. J.
(ed.) *Poets of the 1950s* (Tokyo: Kenkyusha, 1955)
Falck, Colin
'Poetry and Ordinariness', *The New Review*, I:1, April 1974. 'Uncertain Violence', *The New Review*, III:32, November 1976
Feinstein, Elaine
In A Green Eye (London: Goliard Press, 1966). *The Magic Apple Tree* (London: Hutchinson, 1971)
Fenton, James
Terminal Moraine (London: Secker & Warburg, 1972). 'To John Fuller', *The Review*, 29/30, 1972
Ferguson, Peter
'Philip Larkin's *XX Poems:* The Missing Link', *Agenda*, XIV:3, 1976
Ford, Boris
(ed.) *The Pelican Guide To English Literature. Volume 7: The Modern Age* (Harmondsworth: Penguin, 1961; 2nd edition, 1963)
Fraser, G. S.
The Modern Writer and his World (London: Derek Verschoyle, 1953; 2nd edition, Harmondsworth: Penguin, 1964). 'Some Notes on Poetic Diction', *Penguin New Writing*, 37, 1949. 'The Poetry of Thom Gunn', *Critical Quarterly*, III:4, Winter 1961
Fuller, John
Fairground Music (London: Chatto and Windus/Hogarth Press, 1961). *The Tree that Walked* (London: Chatto and Windus/Hogarth Press, 1967). *Cannibals and Missionaries* (London: Secker and Warburg, 1972). *Epistles to Several Persons* (London: Secker and Warburg, 1973). *The Mountain and the Sea* (London: Secker and Warburg, 1975). Review of *Fighting Terms* by Thom Gunn, *The Review*, 1, 1962. Review of *The Visit* by Ian Hamilton, *The Listener*, 4 June 1970. 'To James Fenton', *The Review*, 29/30, 1972
Fuller, Roy
Collected Poems (London, Andre Deutsch, 1962). *Buff* (London: Andre Deutsch, 1965). *New Poems* (London: Andre Deutsch, 1968). *Owls and Artificers* (London: Andre Deutsch, 1971). *Professors and*

Gods (London: Andre Deutsch, 1973). *Tiny Tears* (London: Andre Deutsch, 1973). *From the Joke Shop* (London: Andre Deutsch, 1975). 'Poetry in my Time', *Essays by Divers Hands*, XXXV, 1969. 'Boos of Different Durations', *Thames Poetry*, I:1, 1976. 'The Bum-Bum Game', *Thames Poetry*, I:3, 1977

Grubb, Frederick
A Vision of Reality (London: Chatto and Windus, 1965)

Gunn, Thom
Fighting Terms (Swinford: Fantasy Press, 1954; revised, New York: Hawk's Well Press, 1959; revised, London: Faber, 1962). *The Sense of Movement* (London: Faber, 1957). *My Sad Captains* (London: Faber, 1961). (ed. with Ted Hughes) *Five American Poets* (London: Faber, 1963). (with Ander Gunn) *Positives* (London: Faber, 1967). *Touch* (London: Faber, 1967). (ed.) *Selected Poems of Fulke Greville* (London: Faber, 1968). *Moly* (London: Faber, 1971). (ed.) *Poet to Poet: Ben Jonson* (Harmondsworth: Penguin, 1974). *To the Air* (Boston, Massachusetts: David R. Godine, 1974). *Jack Straw's Castle* (London: Faber, 1976). *The Missed Beat* (Sidcot: The Gruffyground Press, 1976). 'Three Poets', *Listen*, III:1, Winter 1958. 'A Crab', *London Magazine*, New Series, I:11, February 1962. 'Context', *London Magazine*, New Series, I:11, February 1962. 'Tending Bar', *Critical Quarterly*, VI:1, Spring 1964. 'The New Music', *The Listener*, 3 August 1967. 'North Kent', *The Listener*, 22 February 1968. Reply to Questionnaire, *Tracks*, 8, 1970. Reply to Questionnaire on Rhythm, *Agenda*, X:4/XI:1, Autumn-Winter 1972-3. Review of *In the Distance* by Dick Davis, *Thames Poetry*, I:2, 1976

Hamburger, Michael
The Truth of Poetry (London: Weidenfeld and Nicolson, 1970)

Hamilton, Ian
(ed.) *The Modern Poet* (London: Macdonald, 1968). *The Visit* (London: Faber, 1970). *A Poetry Chronicle* (London: Faber, 1973). 'Four Conversations', *London Magazine*, New Series, IV:8, November 1964

Heaney, Seamus
Death of a Naturalist (London: Faber, 1966). *Door into the Dark* (London: Faber, 1969). *A Lough Neagh Sequence* (Manchester: Phoenix, 1969). *Wintering Out* (London: Faber, 1972). *North* (London: Faber, 1975)

Henri, Adrian
'Words and Music', *Poetry Review*, LXII:1, 1971

Holbrook, David
Lost Bearings in English Poetry (London: Vision, 1977)

Hollander, John
   (ed.) *Modern Poetry: Essays in Criticism* (New York: Oxford University Press, 1968)
Homberger, Eric
   The Art of the Real (London: Dent, 1977)
Horovitz, Michael
   (ed.) *Children of Albion* (Harmondsworth: Penguin, 1969)
Hough, Graham
   Image and Experience (London: Duckworth, 1960). *Legends and Pastorals* (London: Duckworth, 1961). *An Essay on Criticism* (London: Duckworth, 1966)
Hughes, Ted
   The Hawk in the Rain (London: Faber, 1957). *Lupercal* (London: Faber, 1960). *Wodwo* (London: Faber, 1967). *Crow* (London: Faber, 1970). *Season Songs* (London: Faber, 1976)
'Hum-Wills, Iago'
   Poems, a broadside (Rushden: Black Turd Press, 1971)
Jackson, Norman
   Beyond the Habit of Sense (London: Villiers, 1968)
Jacobson, Dan
   'Philip Larkin: A Profile', *The New Review,* I:3, June 1974
James, Clive
   'Wolves of Memory', *Encounter,* XLII: 6, June 1974
Jennings, Elizabeth
   Collected Poems (London: Macmillan, 1967). *The Animals' Arrival* (London: Macmillan, 1969). *Lucidities* (London: Macmillan, 1970). *Relationships* (London: Macmillan, 1972). *Growing-Points* (Cheadle: Carcanet, 1975). *Consequently I Rejoice* (Manchester: Carcanet, 1977)
Jones, Peter
   Imagist Poetry (Harmondsworth; Penguin, 1972). *The Garden End* (Manchester: Carcanet, 1978)
Kendrick, George
   Erosions (Manchester: Phoenix, 1971). *Bicycle Tyre in a Tall Tree* (Cheadle: Carcanet, 1974)
Kermode, Frank
   Continuities (London: Routledge and Kegan Paul, 1968). Review of *The Sense of Movement* by Thom Gunn, *Listen,* II:4, Spring 1958
Larkin, Philip
   The North Ship (London: Fortune Press, 1945; London: Faber, 1966). *The Less Deceived* (Hessle: Marvell Press, 1955). *The Whitsun Weddings* (London: Faber, 1964). *All What Jazz* (London: Faber, 1970). (ed.) *The Oxford Book of Twentieth Century English Verse*

(London: Oxford University Press, 1973). *High Windows*, (London: Faber, 1974). 'Breadfruit', *Critical Quarterly*, III:4, Winter 1961. 'Context', *London Magazine*, New Series, I:11, February 1962. Interview, *Tracks*, 1, 1967. 'Heads in the Women's Ward', *New Humanist*, 1, May 1972. Interview, *The Listener*, 12 April 1973

Leavis, F. R.
New Bearings in English Poetry (London: Chatto and Windus, 1932; 2nd edition, 1950)

Lindop, Grevel
Fools' Paradise (Manchester: Carcanet, 1977)

Longley, Michael
Secret Marriages (Manchester: Phoenix, 1968). *No Continuing City* (London: Macmillan, 1969). *An Exploded View* (London: Gollancz, 1973). *Man Lying on a Wall* (London: Gollancz, 1976). Reply to Questionnaire, *The Review*, 29/30, 1972

Lucie-Smith, Edward
(ed.) *The Liverpool Scene* (London: Donald Carroll, 1967). (ed.) *British Poetry since 1945* (Harmondsworth: Penguin, 1970). 'The Tortured Yearned as Well', *Critical Quarterly*, IV:1, Spring 1962

Mahon, Derek
Night-Crossing (London: Oxford University Press, 1968). *Ecclesiastes* (Manchester: Phoenix, 1970). *Lives* (London: Oxford University Press, 1972). *The Snow Party* (London: Oxford University Press, 1975)

May, Derwent
'Some Literary Magazines', *Times Literary Supplement*, 12 February 1970

Melly, George
Revolt into Style (London: Allen Lane, 1970)

Miller, Karl
Writing in England Today (Harmondsworth: Penguin, 1968)

Mole, John
The Instruments (Manchester: Phoenix, 1970). *The Love Horse* (Manchester: Morten, 1973). *A Partial Light* (London: Dent, 1975) *Our Ship* (London: Secker and Warburg, 1977)

Morrison, Blake
'The Movement: A Re-Assessment', *PN Review*, 1, 1976. 'The Movement: A Re-Assessment' (Part 2), *PN Review*, 2, 1977

Olson, Charles
Call Me Ishmael (London: Cape, 1967)

Paulin, Tom
A State of Justice (London: Faber, 1977)

Pearson, Gabriel
'Robert Lowell', *The Review*, 20, 1969

Porter, Peter
Once Bitten, Twice Bitten (Northwood: Scorpion Press, 1961). *Poems Ancient and Modern* (Lowestoft: Scorpion Press, 1964). *A Porter Folio* (Lowestoft: Scorpion Press, 1969). *The Last of England* (London: Oxford University Press, 1970). *Preaching to the Converted* (London: Oxford University Press, 1972) *Living in a Calm Country* (London: Oxford University Press, 1976) 'Opinion', *The Review*, 22, 1970

Pound, Ezra
The Cantos of Ezra Pound (London: Faber, 1954)

Powell, Neil
At the Edge (Manchester: Carcanet, 1977)

Prynne, J. H.
Force of Circumstance (London: Routledge and Kegan Paul, 1962). *Kitchen Poems* (London: Cape Goliard Press, 1968). *The White Stones* (Lincoln: Grosseteste Press, 1969)

'Pygge, Edward'
'Poems', *New Statesman*, 22 June 1973

Press, John
Rule and Energy (London: Oxford University Press, 1963)

Raban, Jonathan
The Society of the Poem (London: Harrap, 1971). Review of *The Victorian Public School* by Brian Simon and Ian Bradley, *New Statesman*, 19 December 1975

Raworth, Tom
The Relation Ship (London: Goliard Press, 1967; 2nd edition, London: Cape Goliard Press, 1969)

Rennie, Neil
Review of *Moly* by Thom Gunn, *London Magazine*, New Series, XI:2, June/July 1971

Robson, Jeremy
(ed.) *The Young British Poets* (London: Chatto and Windus, 1971)

Rosenthal, M. L.
The New Poets (New York: Oxford University Press, 1967)

Schmidt, Michael
(ed. with Grevel Lindop) *British Poetry since 1960* (Oxford: Carcanet, 1972). (ed.) *Ten English Poets* (Manchester: Carcanet, 1976). 'The Poetry of Donald Davie', *Critical Quarterly*, XV:1, Spring 1975

Scott, J. D.
'In the Movement', *Spectator*, 1 October 1954

Scully, James
  (ed.) *Modern Poets on Modern Poetry* (London: Collins, 1966)
Scupham, Peter
  The Small Containers (Manchester: Phoenix, 1972). *The Snowing Globe*
  (Manchester: Morten, 1972). *The Gift* (Richmond: Keepsake Press,
  1973). *Prehistories* (London: Oxford University Press, 1975). *The
  Hinterland* (Oxford: Oxford University Press, 1977)
Sisson, C. H.
  In the Trojan Ditch (Cheadle: Carcanet, 1974). *Anchises* (Manchester:
  Carcanet, 1976). 'Editorial', *PN Review*, 3, 1977
Skelton, Robin
  Review of *Fighting Terms* by Thom Gunn, *Critical Quarterly*, IV:3,
  Autumn 1962
Spiro, Gregory
  (ed.) *Shade Mariners* (Cambridge: Gregory Spiro, Emmanuel College,
  1970)
Stead, C. K.
  The New Poetic (London: Hutchinson, 1964)
Stephens, Alan
  The Sum (Denver: Alan Swallow, 1958)
Swigg, Richard
  'Descending to the Commonplace', *PN Review*, 2, 1977
Thwaite, Anthony
  Home Truths (Hessle: Marvell Press, 1957). *The Owl in the Tree*
  (London: Oxford University Press, 1963). *The Stones of Emptiness*
  (London: Oxford University Press, 1967). *Inscriptions* (London:
  Oxford University Press, 1973). *Poetry Today 1960-1973* (London:
  Longman/British Council, 1973). *A Portion for Foxes* (Oxford: Oxford
  University Press, 1977). 'The Two Poetries', *The Listener*, 5 April
  1973
Timms, David
  Philip Larkin (Edinburgh: Oliver and Boyd, 1973)
Tomlinson, Charles
  The Necklace (Swinford: Fantasy Press, 1955; London: Oxford
  University Press, 1966). *Seeing is Believing* (London: Oxford
  University Press, 1960). *A Peopled Landscape* (London: Oxford
  University Press, 1963). *American Scenes* (London: Oxford University
  Press, 1966). *The Way of a World* (London: Oxford University Press,
  1969). *Written on Water* (London: Oxford University Press, 1972).
  The Way In (London: Oxford University Press, 1974)
Wain, John
  (ed.) *Interpretations* (London: Routledge and Kegan Paul, 1955). *A*

Word Carved on a Sill (London: Routledge and Kegan Paul, 1956). *Weep Before God* (London: Macmillan, 1961). *Wildtrack* (London: Macmillan, 1965). *Letters to Five Artists* (London: Macmillan, 1969). *Feng* (London: Macmillan, 1975). 'Ambiguous Gifts', *Penguin New Writing*, 40, 1950. Review of *Purity of Diction in English Verse* by Donald Davie, *Mandrake*, II:9, 1953

Waterman, Andrew
Living Room (London: Marvell Press, 1974). *From the Other Country* (Manchester: Carcanet, 1977)

Wells, Robert
The Winter's Task (Manchester: Carcanet, 1977)

Williams, Hugo
Symptoms of Loss (London: Oxford University Press, 1965). (ed.) *London Magazine Poems 1961-1966* (London: Alan Ross, 1966). *Sugar Daddy* (London: Oxford University Press, 1970). *Some Sweet Day* (London: Oxford University Press, 1975). Reply to Questionnaire, *The Review*, 29/30, 1972

Winters, Yvor
In Defense of Reason (Denver: Alan Swallow, 1949). *Collected Poems* (Denver: Alan Swallow, 1952). *The Function of Criticism* (Denver: Alan Swallow, 1957). *Forms of Discovery* (Chicago: Alan Swallow, 1967). *Uncollected Essays and Reviews*, ed. Francis Murphy (Chicago: The Swallow Press, 1973)

Wright, David
(ed.) *The Mid-Century: English Poetry 1940-60* (Harmondsworth: Penguin, 1965)

Yeats, W. B.
Collected Poems (London: Macmillan, 1950)